# Storm in a D Cup!

One woman's journey through breast cancer

Debbie Paton

All rights reserved.
ISBN-13: 978-1986176583
ISBN-10: 978-1986176583
Publisher: Debbie Paton Publishing
Address: 1 Holmfield Drive, Raunds, Northants NN9 6PB

# Dedication

I dedicate this blog, which is now my book, to you, Mum.

Love you to the moon and back.

# Reviews

"You have been so brave, Debbie, and are one of the most courageous women I am proud to say I know. Your blog is so informative and really opens your eyes to what actually happens when diagnosed."

"Debbie, I have read all your posts; I have laughed, cried and felt angry for you, but most of all, I have felt the love you have for your family and friends, who are no doubt your tower of strength. I am positive this blog will help thousands of other people going through what you are at the moment, knowing some of the feelings they are experiencing are normal, it would give them strength to plough forward. You are a real inspiration."

"Debbie, you are so brave. I read every blog you wrote. It's hard to believe we were in the same year at school, and how it could have happened to any one of us. With all that is going on in the world, your story brings us all down to earth with a massive bump. Stay strong. You will beat this."

"You write so eloquently about a subject that is clearly very painful for you and those closest to you."

"Inspirational writing from an inspirational lady."

# Acknowledgements

I would like to thank all the medical staff who have been involved with my care in the last year or so, including my consultant, Miss Alex Knight, the oncologists, radiographers, the breast nurses at Kettering General Hospital and all of the breast care team.

I want to thank Glennis Hooper and her wonderful charity Crazy Hats for supporting me through this journey and for introducing me to so many new friends who have become a permanent part of my life. I am now on the committee of the charity and I hope to be able to give back some of the support and care I've received in the past. A group of us are in the process of putting together a calendar for 2019 in support of the charity, called Dare to Bare to be Breast Aware.

I couldn't have got through this without the support of my wonderful family and friends. I am truly blessed to have the most caring and thoughtful husband with the patience of a saint. He saw me through the darkest of days and was possibly the only one who saw me at my most vulnerable. He never stopped picking me up and putting me back on the road to positivity. You are my rock, my port in the storm.

My girls, Georgia and Phoebe, I am so immensely proud of the way you coped with the situation especially during important exam seasons. Your strength gave me strength, and I want you both to know how much you each mean to me. You two are the best things I have ever done in my life, and I sometimes feel I could pop with pride.

I want to thank my mum and dad for not going to pieces and staying strong to help me push ahead, my sister for picking up the pieces when I had the occasional meltdown and for taking the time to give me a makeover on one of my lowest days.

Being ill has actually made me realise what a wonderful family, extended family and close friends I have. I feel blessed and wish I could thank them all by name, but that would take another book.

I think the most important person in most girls' lives are their mums, and I am no exception. I lost my mum in May 2017, but I want to acknowledge her for being the person who taught me so many positive things, to follow my dreams and to strive to be the best at whatever I did. I hope the publication of this book would have made you proud.

Debbie Paton
February 2018

# About the Book

Storm in a D Cup! is a blow-by-blow account of Debbie Paton's journey through breast cancer. It is a candid account of the year between her initial diagnosis and her full recovery.

When she was first diagnosed, Debbie wrote notes in a diary, but her daughter Georgia dragged her into the 21st century by convincing her to write a blog that could be shared with a wider audience.

The blog soon became Debbie's cathartic writing. It gave her the freedom to express the rollercoaster of emotions as they happened, the good, the bad and the irrational. She shared her entries on social media for her friends and family to follow – it took the pressure off endless update phone calls!

This is a no holds barred account of the mix of emotions, the highs and lows of the journey. It is not about doom and gloom, but rather the realities of the journey and the experiences Debbie had along the way. It is at times poignant and highly sensitive, at others, filled with laughter and fun. It was a year that shaped her life into something different.

It is Debbie's hope that her experiences can help others by alleviating some of the fear surrounding a breast cancer diagnosis. If she could have read a similar blog before starting her own journey, Debbie feels certain she would've been far less fearful of what lay ahead. Yes, everyone's path is different, but there are elements of her experience that will resonate with others in the same position.

## The Journey Begins

Friday, 11 March 2016

2:21 p.m.

Today I had a routine mammogram at the Nene Park Outpatients Clinic in Irthlingborough. I met a friend who was coming out of the mobile unit, and I had a quick catch-up with her. I was in there for just a few minutes, and I was told my results would arrive in the next 2 weeks.

Now, I'm the kind of person who will always attend routine health checks, but little did I know this custom of mine would prove to be such a positive for me.

About a week later I received a letter from the hospital asking me to return for more tests. There was little more than that in the letter. I discussed it with my mum, and we both convinced ourselves that maybe the images were not great and they just needed to repeat them to be sure everything was okay.

# The Tests Begin

## Friday, 24 March 2016

I was called back to the Kettering General Hospital Breast Unit for further investigation. My husband, Gus, came with me for support – thank goodness he did. I wasn't expecting it to be so intense and feel so serious. I thought the tests would be simple, and I'd be out of the hospital quickly. I can remember thinking that the staff, though very supportive, had grave expressions.

The procedure was a further mammogram, an ultrasound, then 4 biopsies were taken plus an aspiration, which is when a fine needle is inserted to draw off a small amount of fluid from the lymph gland. All of this was explained to us by the breast nurse before the procedures began.

An abnormality that was found in my right breast required further investigation. The mammogram was as expected, but the ultrasound seemed to go on for ages. A local anaesthetic was put into my right breast before the biopsies were taken. The first one was a shock, and it made me jump.

I was asked if I'd like more painkillers, but I refused and said that now I knew what to expect, I would be okay. The breast nurse, Anne, sat with me throughout, holding an ice pack to my right breast to reduce any bruising or swelling afterwards.

The aspiration was taken from a lymph cell with a needle. It was painful but manageable, like a needle scratching at the inside of me. I knew from this point on, something was drastically wrong.

Anne spoke to us afterwards and explained the results would take 2 weeks. As it was Good Friday and Easter Monday that weekend, the results might take longer than usual. I felt sick because I thought I would have the results sooner with less time to worry. We were going away on holiday from 4–11 April, so we changed the appointment to 15 April. We chose to go with this because I still hoped it would be nothing to worry about, even though I had a feeling of dread too, if that makes any sense?

I'm fit and healthy, and I do my best to look after myself by walking the dogs every day, practising yoga and regular weight training. There hadn't been any lumps, bumps or changes in my breast, so why worry?

# The Optimistic Phone Call

## Thursday, 31 March 2016

I had a phone call from the Breast Unit asking if I'd like to take a cancellation appointment the next day at 2 p.m. as Miss Knight, the consultant, had a space. I agreed because I thought it must be good news, and they wanted me to go away on holiday with the knowledge that everything was okay, right?

# The Darkest Day

## Friday, 1 April 2016

Today was the day I was told I have breast cancer, a Stage 2 Lobular cancer that was 7 cm in diameter. I was told it's a sneaky cancer that hides itself well and would have only been picked up by a mammogram. There are no obvious signs such as a lump or a change in shape of the breast as with many other types of breast cancer; something which I think all women should be aware of.

It was like being harpooned against the wall – I was winded! How could it be me? I'm fit and healthy. I haven't felt anything unusual or felt poorly. I'm crying as I write all of this down; it still feels so surreal even though I'm writing this 5 weeks after having been told everything. How? Why? The questions poured out. The consultant said it could have started 6, 12, 18 months ago, there was no way of knowing. Thank goodness for the routine test was all I could think.

Miss Knight, my consultant (who is an absolute dream to have as a consultant, it's like talking to a best friend. I can never repay her for what she's given me – the chance of life), explained the strands of treatment that I would be looking at.

Mastectomy – that was a shock. I have to lose my whole breast to survive this. Due to the type of cancer, the only option I have is removal as it grows like a web rather than a mass.

Chemotherapy – possibly depending on what she removes and whether it has gone into my lymph nodes – again, shock! Lymph nodes? What does that mean? I've learnt a lot since this day and I now know that the lymph system is the barrier before the cancer can travel anywhere else in the body. Oh my goodness, what if it has spread?

Radiotherapy – to my chest wall and possibly under arm.

Medication – for up to 5 years depending on where I am in the menopause stage.

Reconstruction – what? Forget it! That's all I could think, all I wanted was for this nasty disease to be cut out of my body so I could live. The way I look is not my priority – I said this out loud, and she seemed to respect me for this because lots of women are concerned about body image at this stage. Nothing could be further from my mind.

Miss Knight said she called me in today as she felt it was unfair to let me go on holiday without the facts. She was very straight forward in her approach, which I liked. I wanted to know the facts and possible outcomes. She reassured me by saying yes I had cancer, but that it was her job to make sure that I died of something else in 40–50 years time. I liked her approach, and I had every faith in her abilities from the very start.

She said we could go away and think about the options and then arrange another appointment to see her. Gus and I both agreed we needed to get on with this and not give the cancer a chance to keep going. She said it wasn't an aggressive cancer, but that didn't reassure me in any way. I was walking around with this 'gremlin' and I wanted it gone.

She said the first available surgery date would be 14 April. For me that was a good omen – it would have been my grandad's 115th birthday if he was still with us and his name was Bill Knight, the same surname as the consultant – a coincidence? Fate? Who knows, but I was up for going ahead. Don't get me wrong, if this could have just been a cruel April Fool's Day joke then I couldn't have been happier, but it wasn't. Time was of the essence as far as I was concerned. Let's do it.

Miss Knight said that as I was fit and healthy, young, with no underlying health issues and wasn't on any medications, then I should recover quickly.

She shook our hands and left the room. Anne the breast nurse took over.

I broke down at the thought of telling the girls; I was about to shatter their lives for a while, and I didn't want to have to do that. Anne was very supportive and talked us through everything. Time didn't matter, and at no point did I feel rushed or that I was asking silly questions.

I had my pre-operation assessment while I was there, too, as the consultant had told us to go away on our holiday to Majorca and to eat, drink and be merry. We were due to fly home on the 11 April and I would be in hospital 3 days later. There was no time for worrying.

# Going Home

## Friday, 1 April 2016

We drove home afterwards and stopped off at a McDonald's to buy some coffee and to talk about how we were going to tell the girls. We decided to keep it to ourselves for that night, and we'd tell them the next day.

Gus wondered whether we should tell them on holiday, but we decided against this – I wanted them to be able to shout, cry, slam doors and express their emotions however they wanted, in the confines of their own home.

That evening was awful. I cooked dinner for the three of us, Gus, Phoebe (aged 14) and me. I picked at mine and when Phoebe asked what was wrong, I said I didn't much like the pork I had made. If only she knew...

Amazingly, I slept well. I was absolutely exhausted.

# The Most Difficult Day Ever

## Saturday, 2 April 2016

Phoebe went to work at 9 a.m. We'd decided it would be best to tell the girls together when she got home from work at 2 p.m. Fate, however, decided to take a different turn.

I had been on the phone to my mum trying to sort out a time to go and see them. Georgia (aged 17), had detected a subtle change in my voice, and she asked what was wrong. When I said nothing, she kept pressing me and got tearful, almost hysterical. She thought my dad was ill or had died, but I assured her that, no, that wasn't the case. It wasn't that bad.

Immediately, she asked about my test results. She knew I had to go back but didn't know when I would get the results. I had to tell her. It was an awful thing to have to do because I knew I was about to break her heart. It still makes me cry thinking about it. She sobbed but then asked what Stage it was. Stage? What did she know about Stages?

She told me she'd researched it all when she knew I needed to go back to the clinic – what an amazing child. When I told her it was Stage 2 she almost collapsed with relief. I still had no real understanding of the Stages and Grades but she seemed to know everything. She brightened immediately because she said I'd be okay, and I would recover. Georgia said she was dreading me saying that it was Stage 4 or worse, 5! I am absolutely in awe of this wonderful teenager I've helped to shape – she is amazing, as is her younger sister.

Gus said he was proud of the way I had explained it to her. I did it the only way I knew how, really.

Next was Phoebe when she got home from work. Georgia and Gus stayed in the room while I explained it all over again to her. She cried and hugged me, just wanting to be reassured there was a light at the end of the tunnel. I consider Phoebe to be the 'deeper' of the two girls, and I've been concerned she might bottle things up and not talk about how she feels, but this hasn't been the case. The weeks that followed have been joyful, at times, and this has brought us all so much closer.

I asked my sister to come round at 3 p.m. I told her and she was very upset but relieved I wasn't telling her I had cervical cancer, which was something we'd talked about a few days earlier.

Next were my mum and dad. Mum broke down and started to say it should have been her, she'd had her life. I explained that's not how it works, and I needed her to be strong and supportive for me. Dad didn't say much. I guess it's awkward talking to your grown-up daughter about such a sensitive subject. He said he felt I was in the best hands, and I'd come through this. They have continued to be supportive and listened when I needed them.

Now for everyone else. I couldn't face lots of phone calls to the many friends and family I didn't even realise I had, so instead I decided to send a carefully worded text message to some and a Facebook message to others. The outpouring of love and kindness that followed was overwhelming for me, and I still can't believe so many people care about me. I'm just me, no one special. I am so humbled by the enormity of affection and regard I have received.

# Holiday

## 4–11 April 2016 – Majorca

Our holiday was an amazing week away with my incredible, perfect, wonderful husband and daughters. There were a few dark moments for me; moments when I thought, 'Will this be the last time I do...' but on the whole it was a very special week.

We walked for miles, talked, ate, drank and enjoyed each other's company more than we ever have before, and I think this feeling will never change. When you think you might have the slightest chance of losing something forever, it makes you appreciate things a thousand times more.

Gus rang his mum and her partner, Barrie, before we arrived in Majorca to let them know the situation so they would be prepared, and we weren't dropping a bombshell the moment we met up. We went to see them for a couple of days at their place in the hills. The girls stayed at their villa, and we stayed in a little boutique hotel in the village. It's a quaint little hotel with so much charm. It was good to have some time on our own just looking out from the balcony, taking in the vastness of the sea, which was so peaceful and beautiful. We had a fantastic time and although there were moments of seriousness, we were able to lighten up most of the week and enjoy the time together.

Making memories is what life is all about. These 'photographs of the past' are what spur us all on in times when we feel low or are experiencing any hardship in life.

There have been many times over the past decade or so when I've actually said, 'If I died tomorrow, I would die happy,' because of all the wonderful memories I have with my family and friends, and for the opportunities I've had to do things and the wonderful places I've had the chance to visit. I have never said those words in a flippant manner but, boy, have the last few days made me think how much I want to live and make more of those wonderful memories.

# Back to Work

## Tuesday, 12 April 2016

Reality hits home! Everyone in the house got up and went off to work and school as normal, but today was not going to be a normal day for me.

I am a Specialist Drugs Worker for the Youth Offending Team, a position I absolutely love. I get to spend time with young people who have sometimes made the wrong choices; they are not necessarily 'bad' people, they've had a difficult time growing up or fell in with the wrong crowd. I feel privileged to be able to try to help them and give them accurate information about substances they are, or have been using. I sit and listen to their views and their reasons for doing what they do. I'm not there to judge them; just to try to steer them in the right direction and make sure they stay on the right side of the law.

However, today was a bit different. I wasn't in the office for long. It was too much for me; the gravity of what I was up against hit me. The last time I'd been at work I had no idea there was anything wrong with me, and I'd been looking forward to my holiday.

I managed to get a few administrative tasks completed for my boss before deciding to leave for the day. I couldn't cope with having to talk to my colleagues about what was coming up for me. I could feel the surge of tears, and I needed to escape and be on my own for a bit.

Luckily, I have a very understanding boss (plus a great team of people), and I was able to leave discreetly without anyone really noticing. I drove away sobbing. I felt like my life and work would never be the same again.

Fear of the unknown is such a powerful topic for the mind.

# Reality Bites

## Wednesday, 13 April 2016

Today it started to get real. I had an appointment at the Kettering General Hospital Nuclear Physics Department. It sounded like I was about to enter Doctor Who territory. I had built this up in my mind to be much worse than it turned out to be in the end.

I had to have some routine blood tests done first. The procedure at the Nuclear Physics Department was to inject a radioactive substance into the affected breast so that when the consultant operates, she is able to identify and cherry pick which lymph nodes to remove by adding blue dye – how clever!

It's the idea of this procedure that scares me most; the lymph nodes need to be tested for the presence of cancer cells. The original biopsy tests showed no cancer cells in the lymph cell they tested, but the consultant told us there was a 50:50 chance the cancer had spread to the lymph nodes. Knowing this was quite frightening for me – if it had travelled there then where else might it have snaked its tentacles?

The procedure itself wasn't painful, maybe a little bit uncomfortable, but there was nothing for me to have been anxious about. I've given blood for years and it wasn't even on a par with that. Giving blood is a breeze.

Gus and I had lunch at a favourite pub on the way home. We sat in the garden, the sun was shining and everything seemed well with the world.

The darker clouds appeared later on that day when reality really began to bite. A friend called round and cried. I held it together and tried to reassure her when inside, all I wanted to do was to scream and cry myself.

I spent the evening with Gus and the girls and got an early night. Strangely, I slept well and didn't wake all night. I was dreading the next day, but I knew there was no way out of this other than the option I'd been given. Life deals its cards.

# D Day

## Thursday, 14 April 2016

## D day had arrived

I got up and dressed then spoke to the girls and reassured them I would be fine.

I checked to make sure I had everything I needed – pyjamas, toiletries, books, magazines, my tarot 'Sun' card (my sister-in-law had completed a reading for me a few days before and was elated because of the positivity connected with it. She said the significance of the Sun card was that everything was going to be okay), mobile phone, etc.

We drove to the hospital at 7 a.m. It was a good job Gus was driving because I'm pretty sure I would've been hurtling at 100 mph in the opposite direction if I'd been at the wheel.

We arrived, and I remember taking a big breath and thinking, let's get on with this.

We went up to the ward, where I'd been given a room of my own, Room 14, more good vibes. Room 14 on 14 April (my grandad's birthday) and a consultant who shared his surname.

I had visits from the consultant, the anaesthetist and the ward nurse. All of them were extremely professional and put me at my ease. It almost felt as if I was there for a pleasurable purpose. Nothing seemed too much trouble, and no question deemed too silly.

The anaesthetist asked about the surgery I had 14 years ago to remove my gall bladder. I said I'd been fine and hadn't been sick afterwards, but that I was concerned about it. He thought it odd that I worried so much given that I've never been sick after a general anaesthetic. The truth is, vomiting is one of my fears in life, and I'll do anything to avoid it. My mum says that as a child I would try to run if I witnessed someone throwing up.

When 9 a.m. arrived and a theatre nurse came to collect me, it was hard to walk away from Gus, but I knew this was it and I had to go. All sorts of things go through your mind at this point, irrational thoughts like, 'What if I don't make it?' and 'What if I never see him and the girls again?' He squeezed me tight, and we parted company.

It's surreal that you walk into the operating theatre and get onto your own operating table. Everyone in the room is asking questions or attaching pads or stickers to your body. I don't know how many times I told them which breast to remove even though there was a bloody big black marker pen arrow pointing to it. Better to be safe than sorry I guess.

The anaesthetist held a tiny mask over my nose and said it might make me feel a bit dizzy. It did for a moment and that was the last thing I remember. Two and a half hours later I was being woken up by a nurse called Clive. I was having a lovely dream and wanted him to go away.

I felt fine – no sickness or nausea at all. Within half an hour I was back in my room on the ward being offered a cup of tea. I gingerly drank the black tea in case I needed to throw up, but there was no need, I was fine. A nurse asked if I'd like some toast or a sandwich. I wasn't too sure and nibbled on an extra strong mint instead. I nibbled through two, and there was still no sickness or nausea, so the nurse brought me a ham sandwich.

My consultant came to see me at about 1 p.m. She told me everything had gone to plan and that if I could eat, I could go home today. Music to my ears, I could go home.

Gus had been ringing since noon, so they told him he could come to see me. I think he was pleasantly surprised to find me sitting up in bed, drinking another cup of tea. I ate some of the sandwich and gave Gus the rest. A white bread ham sandwich wouldn't normally be my food of choice.

The saline drip was removed, and I was able to get to the bathroom unaided. I decided to put on my own pyjamas and get out of the hospital gown. It was tricky and my chest wall felt sore when I raised my arm, but it wasn't particularly painful. The wound was covered with a square compression plaster and looked clean and neat.

I was on half hourly observation for the first few hours, then hourly from 5 p.m. I left the hospital at 7 p.m., relieved I could go home and sleep in my own bed with my own family nearby. The consultant was happy with my progress. My hope was that all the 'nasty bits' had been completely removed, and I was now cancer-free. I wouldn't know for sure for a few weeks as the tumour needed to be tested, and the removed lymph nodes had to be tested for any cancerous cells.

The staff at the hospital were all fantastic and my brief stay was uneventful. The discharge nurse was perhaps the most negative part of the experience. She wouldn't make eye contact with me throughout her form filling and was dismissive when I asked about a 'softy' to go home with. A 'softy' is a soft prosthesis to put inside a bra to mimic a breast. She said she didn't know anything about it, and that I would have to ring in the morning. Luckily, I'm not the sort of person to go to pieces, but I felt she was rather insensitive considering what I'd just gone through. Maybe she had things going on in her own life, or she'd had a bad day, though I doubt it could have been as bad as mine!

We came home and did normal stuff. We ate dinner, watched Emmerdale and chatted about family things. I can't tell you how wonderful it felt to do these normal little family things. I was home, the 'gremlin' had been banished, and I was ALIVE!

I took paracetamol and ibuprofen before turning in. My bed felt better than ever that night. It was uncomfortable to turn over, and I spent most of the night in one position, but it was home and there's nothing like it. I only woke once in the night, which was pretty good going.

This was the start of a new chapter.

Hospital 14 April 2016

# Recovery Begins

## Friday, 15 April 2016

## Day 1 of recovery

I am amazed by how well I feel. I'm uncomfortable but not in pain, thanks to paracetamol and ibuprofen.

One of the breast nurses called me early this morning to ask if I was able to go in today. They had forgotten to give me the blood thinning injections I needed as I had flown 3 days prior to surgery. I was also able to ask about the 'softy.'

At the hospital I was shown how to inject myself into the fat of my tummy. I would have to do this for 28 consecutive days. I was quite shocked as I was expecting it to be a one-off injection. Though I was nervous of injecting myself, it wasn't as bad as I expected and I felt it wouldn't be a problem to do at home for the duration.

One of the nurses helped me find the right size 'softy.' It was a bit alien. I'd been used to having my own breast since I was a teenager. The nurse was really helpful and gave me three to take away to use until I was able to have a prosthesis fitted. She made me an appointment for Thursday, 12 May.

My mum, dad, sister and brother-in-law visited today. It was so lovely to see them, and I think they were all quite shocked to see me looking so well. There were phone calls, texts and Facebook messages from other family members and friends. It's so heart-warming to know you are loved.

Today we tried to have a quiet day at home together. The girls went to school as usual, and in the evening we all had dinner together and enjoyed each other's company.

# A Busy Saturday

## Saturday, 16 April 2016

Another good night's sleep. The pain is lessening, and there's just a burning sensation if I over-stretch my right arm.

The breast nurse had given me some tips for bathing and showering to keep the dressing as dry as possible. So, armed with a roll of cling film, Georgia and I set about making me shower proof. It was pretty comical. She held a length of cling film while I twirled around until I was wrapped like a chicken fillet ready for the freezer! It still makes me chuckle to think about it. Thank goodness I hadn't had two sons, or I'd have had to rope Gus in to help. I was able to shower and even managed to wash my own hair. I felt really good about being able to do this. I sat on the bed and dried my hair. The battered and bruised part of my body didn't seem quite real somehow; as if it wasn't me in the reflection.

Phoebe went away today to complete her bronze Duke of Edinburgh practice walk with the school. She was all prepared, and I really didn't have to help her with anything. It was hard to let her go. I want to be close to my family and never let them out of my sight. She took her phone, so she could stay in contact with me. I'm so proud of her.

I had quite a few visitors today. The phone and the doorbell seemed to ring constantly, and I was pretty exhausted by teatime. Gus made me go to bed and have a lie down for an hour. It was the best advice he could have given me.

We had friends over for a takeaway in the evening, which I thoroughly enjoyed. I stayed up quite late but felt fine and by the time I went to bed, I fell asleep quickly.

# Bruising and Swelling

## Sunday, 17 April 2016

A lazy Sunday at home. Phoebe came back from her Duke of Edinburgh weekend and we had a delicious family dinner together. This is what life is all about.

I have begun to notice quite a bit of swelling, but I put it down to wearing an underwire bra yesterday. It has caused a lot of additional bruising, so I will be keeping a close eye on it.

I'm worrying now about the swelling and bruising. Did I cause this by wearing the bra? Did I walk too far when we took the dogs out? I did get out of breath and had to stop a few times. I hate feeling like this, especially when I can usually walk for miles and miles with no ill effects. Will I ever be able to do that again?

Georgia even asked me if the consultant had actually removed the whole breast. She wondered if she had only removed part of it as she said it almost looked like it was growing back. That's how swollen it was becoming!

I'm used to being fit and healthy all the time. I play badminton for 2 hours at a time, I go to yoga classes, I was up to lifting 47.5 kg for my dead lift training before the operation, and I walk the dogs for miles. These are all things I've taken for granted – am I expecting too much, too soon?

# Hole in the Ceiling

## Wednesday, 20 April 2016

Gus went back to work today. I wasn't looking forward to this at all as he's been such a great support for me, and I haven't had to lift a finger. If I tried to do anything I shouldn't have been doing, he'd been there to stop me. I even lied when I made the bed one morning and said Georgia had helped me, but it backfired on me because she didn't backup my story. Serves me right.

This was the very morning the bath decided to spring a leak and soak the kitchen downstairs. It was at this point that I really understood something; I wasn't feeling my usual self, emotionally. I went into meltdown, left a voicemail for Gus, sobbing, and replied to my sister's text with much the same woe!

My sister turned into Wonder Woman and came straight round, sorted me out and got on with clearing up the kitchen. She got me to call the insurance company and made me tell them about my health situation. I found all this really difficult, but it had a positive ending – the plumber was at my door within the hour and the leak was mended.

Drama over. There's a small hole in the ceiling, which could easily be fixed. If only people could be fixed that easily.

# Overwhelmed

## Friday, 22 April 2016

I've been home alone for 3 days now, and I haven't had a minute to be bored or to dwell on any negatives because I've had so many visitors. I'm overwhelmed by the number of people I know and the extent of their love and affection. I've even been out for breakfast with some of my work colleagues – they're a gregarious bunch of people, and I do miss them.

The swelling and bruising don't seem to be getting any better. I decided to call the Breast Unit to ask their advice. When I explained about the bruising, the burning sensation, and the swelling, they said they wanted to see me in clinic. It was 4:30 p.m. on Friday, so I had no way of getting there in time today and had been given an appointment for Monday. I was told to take it easy and to continue with the painkillers. I hadn't been unduly concerned up to this point, but now I knew I really needed to look after myself.

The house is full of flowers, and I mean full. I have been a florist for more years than I care to remember, but I've never seen a house so full of them – I was running out of vases. They are all so beautiful, and they make me very happy. I love flowers, they are one of the greatest beauties on earth. The scent of fragrant freesias, earthy hyacinths and heady lilies filled the air for days.

# Relaxing Weekend

## Saturday, 23 April 2016

I tried to have a relaxing weekend and not do too much to aggravate the swelling. Gus has taken over all the cooking, cleaning, shopping and washing, with the help of the girls. I have a spick and span house, food in the cupboards and a non-existent ironing pile. He has cooked some tasty meals and has been researching all the 'good' foods to help with the fight against cancer. The girls complained about the amount of turmeric that keeps appearing in our meals, especially the radioactive-coloured mash! This is because turmeric adds a subtle taste, but it also gives a vibrant change to the colour, making the usual pale cream mash into a glowing terracotta.

I invested in a good quality juicer today. I have a feeling our fruit and veg bill is going to go through the roof now.

# Appointment

## Monday, 25 April 2016

I had an appointment with Miss Knight, my consultant, at Kettering General Hospital.

She asked if I had removed the dressing, but I told her I hadn't needed to. When she asked if it was okay for her to do it, I said it was fine but that I was nervous about seeing what was underneath. As she removed it, I saw the breast nurse wince.

The consultant, ever the professional, was brilliant. She explained I had a haematoma, a bleed into the wound area, and that's what had caused the swelling. She was upset because it was probably caused by the blood thinning injections, which she hadn't thought necessary because I'd only been on a short, two hour flight.

Unfortunately, this complication would mean going back into hospital for an operation to clear the haematoma and clean the area. My heart sank. Another general anaesthetic and being opened up again. I had been brave and almost nonchalant about events up until now, but now I felt frightened. I thought the worst part, the operation, was done and dusted, but now I had to go back under anaesthetic again.

I felt such a fool. Why hadn't I realised earlier that this wasn't normal and done something about it? The consultant was very reassuring and said, 'Why would you know what was normal? When did you ever have a mastectomy?' That made me smile because she was right, how would I have anything to compare it with? That aside, I was really disappointed and felt like the stuffing had been knocked out of me again.

Miss Knight asked me to go back in on Thursday, 28 April. She said it would be a simple 20 minute operation, and I'd be able to go home the same day. She also said she'd hurry along the test results of the lymph nodes. If a full node clearance was necessary, she would do this at the same time, so I didn't need to potentially have a third operation. Maybe this was a positive, I couldn't decide.

Thursday, 28 April was the date of the Bryan Adams concert in Nottingham. I was supposed to have been going and staying overnight in a hotel with my good friend, Lucy. We had planned a day of shopping, chatting, eating and doing girly stuff before the concert. Neither of us got to the concert as we were both recovering from operations. Luckily, the tickets were passed on, so others enjoyed the concert.

# Relief

## Wednesday, 27 April 2016

I tried to fill the next few days with friends and family, lunches out and anything to take my mind off what was to come next. We had been told to expect a call today to confirm the lymph node tests. I couldn't eat or settle all day. By 4 p.m. there had been no call, so I decided to ring them myself, but it went to answerphone. I was distraught. I needed to know, so I could mentally prepare myself for tomorrow.

I got through at 4:26 p.m. They close at 4:30 p.m., so you can imagine my angst. The breast nurse said she'd been in the meeting and went to get her notes. Those were the longest two minutes. She came back and said Miss Knight wanted to speak with me in the morning, but that there was no need for a full node clearance. I'd been gripping Gus's hand so hard while I was on the phone; I so wanted this news. Apparently, of the 4 lymph nodes that were removed, 3 were clear of cancer and the other had a micro metastasis cancer cell. It wasn't necessary to remove all the lymph nodes, as this microscopic cell would be killed by my own immune system, or the radiotherapy.

It was like we'd won the lottery. We laughed and cried and jumped around the kitchen. I could settle myself to what needed to be done tomorrow – a simple operation, and I'd be home again.

Georgia was going to a concert in London with her boyfriend and staying over. She would be away when I went off to hospital this time, and that didn't feel good. I hated having to reassure her over the phone. Both of the girls have had a lot to cope with in the last few weeks, and I'm so proud of the way they've conducted themselves. They are a part of the cement that holds this family together. I couldn't have wished for better children. They are incredible to me.

# D Day Part 2

Thursday, 28 April 2016

## D Day Part 2 had arrived

Strangely, I didn't feel as apprehensive this time around. I guess this may have been because of the good news yesterday.

We arrived at the hospital at 7:30 a.m. as planned and went to the Day Care centre. It was apparent this was going to be a quick in and out procedure.

The consultant came in to see me and sat swinging her legs on my bed. She feels like a friend rather than my consultant. She explained all about the biopsies and what that meant in the future. She said I would need some radiotherapy to the chest wall and possibly under my arm. She also told me the oncologist felt I didn't need chemotherapy, but ultimately it would be up to me. If I felt it would give me an 'insurance policy' for the future, then it would be wise to go ahead with it.

I was due to be the first one into theatre, but there was a patient with an allergy to latex who needed to be operated on first, so I'd be next in line.

The minutes and hours ticked by. I read a magazine and goodness knows how many chapters of my book. I was all ready to go, with my gown and fetching bottle green support socks and red slipper socks, all hospital issue. The theatre nurse eventually came for me at 11:40 a.m. I was asleep by 11:50 a.m. and back in my hospital bed by 12:45 p.m. It's a surreal experience being put out; the time has gone and yet I have no recollection of any of it.

When the nurse in recovery woke me up, she told me I'd said the strangest thing. Apparently, I'd shouted, 'Punch Clive.' I laughed as I explained that a nurse called Clive had woken me from the operation 2 weeks ago while I'd been in the middle of a dream – poor Clive!

My consultant came to see me a little later, and I was discharged before 4 p.m. By 4:30 p.m. I was back in my own lounge at home. Incredible!

I can't believe how much more comfortable I feel already. They have put a pressure dressing on top of the waterproof dressing, and it's very tight, but it only has to stay on for 24 hours.

It's so comforting to be at home again and begin the recuperation process once more.

# Our Wedding Anniversary

## Saturday, 30 April 2016

It's been 2 days since the operation and I'm feeling surprisingly well. It's only now that I realise something was definitely amiss after the first operation. I am a bit sore, but other than that, I'm fine, and I haven't even needed much pain relief. After I removed the pressure dressing yesterday, it was obvious I'd lost the whole breast. I'm as flat as a pancake. It's strange, as I've spent much of my adult life wishing I was a little less well-endowed, but I didn't want it to be quite this extreme. Never mind, life deals its cards, and I am here and alive. What else could matter?

It's our 23rd wedding anniversary today. Where did the time go? I didn't have the best start in the romance stakes as my first marriage began at the tender age of 20 (when you think you know everything), and ended at 22. Gus and I married after a brief 10-month courtship, but during that spell we only managed about 7 weeks in each other's company as he was stationed in Paderborn, Germany, and I was in the UK teaching floristry at Moulton College.

Twenty-three years and two gorgeous daughters later, here we are. I never want this partnership to come to an end, ever, though I know one day it will have to. The last few weeks have made me look at mortality more directly. I know it's pretty unlikely we'll both go to sleep one night and both not wake up in the morning. Sorry if I'm sounding morbid. I don't feel morbid; I'm just being realistic and hopeful.

# Bloody Disease

## Sunday, 1 May 2016

Today was the Mayor's Show in Raunds. Phoebe and Fizz, our 2-year-old Parson Jack Russell terrier, took part in a dog agility demonstration at the show. I watched with my friend Lucy, and Gus. Seeing how good Phoebe was with Fizz, how they seemed to know what each other was thinking, I felt like my heart would burst with pride at such a close bond.

Lucy received the news that she has lung cancer on the day of my last operation, and this was the first time we'd met since then. We've known each since school but have only really been in touch again in the last few years. Neither of us can quite believe we've both been diagnosed with this bloody disease within days of one another. It's a cruel coincidence.

We sat in silence for a lot of the afternoon, just lost in our own thoughts, watching the afternoon's proceedings. It's at times like this in life that you realise how special your friends really are.

The last few days have been busy with visitors and trying to get my head around other friends' illnesses. I don't know if you are more alert to things once you've been diagnosed, but I feel as if I'm surrounded by cancer; it's in the papers, on the TV and generally in the news.

Since I've been diagnosed, I've heard of three other dear friends who've been diagnosed with different cancers. They are all good people and it's distressing to know they have such difficult roads to travel back to good health.

I've been thinking about how cancer seems to pick on 'good' people. Maybe the people I think of as not so good, evil even, who inflict pain and anguish on others and animals, maybe those people do suffer, but I don't hear about them. They probably don't have the huge support network of family and friends some of us are so lucky to have. No one deserves to suffer.

# Treatment Information

## Thursday, 5 May 2016

We spent 2 hours with the breast nurse today. The purpose of this was for her to explain the treatment going forward. She also gave me information about my individual cancer and the tests that have been done post-surgery. She confirmed my cancer was invasive lobular breast cancer, there was only one tumour 8 cm long, and it was Stage 2, Grade 2. Initially I had been told the tumour was 7 cm, but after its removal and investigation it was found to be 8 cm.

I've done a lot of surfing online to get a better understanding of my type of cancer. Lobular cancer is one of the commonest forms of breast cancer, and it develops in the milk ducts of the breast, which is why it's particularly difficult to detect without a mammogram, and it doesn't manifest itself as a lump or a change in breast shape. Stage 2 means that the cancer is treatable and even curable while the Grade is the aggressiveness of the tumour. Grade 2 is one of the less aggressive types.

There was 1 lymph node that showed a micro metastasis (cancer cell) out of the 4 removed. Vascular invasion was negative. It was oestrogen receptor positive but HER 2 Receptor negative. In layman's terms this means I won't need further surgery. However, I will need some radiotherapy to the chest wall and maybe under the arm. I will also possibly need a course of chemotherapy, but this isn't certain at the moment and I will need to talk with the oncologist. I'll receive an appointment to see him in the next few weeks.

I was informed that I wouldn't see my consultant surgeon for another 12 months, something I see as a positive. She's done her bit – saved my life. I can't thank her enough. She's given me the chance to carry on living.

# Difficult Conversations

## Monday, 9 May 2016

The last few days have been full and busy. We've had meals out with friends and went to a dance show Phoebe was part of. I'm so proud of the way she's carried on through this and been able to perform; she's a star.

I spent the morning sorting out important stuff like life insurance, the mortgage and holiday insurance as most companies have to be notified of a change in health. I found all of this quite hard as I had to tell a stranger each time that I had a cancer diagnosis – powerful stuff and very emotional. Everyone I spoke to was very understanding and patient, and they were able to talk me through all the options and look for the best solutions. People are generally very kind, aren't they? Especially in these kinds of situations.

One of the hardest things I did today was cancelling my blood donor appointment. The guy I spoke to was very empathetic, he asked about my illness and then had to tell me I wouldn't ever be able to donate blood again. I felt my lip tremble and the tears start to trickle down my face. I'd given almost fifty pints, and I was looking forward to achieving that goal. He turned my negative into a positive by making me reflect on the forty plus lives I have probably already helped or saved. That made me cry a little more.

I have loved being a blood donor, and I am encouraging my daughters to do the same when they are able to. It has been such a privilege to be able to give something that will help another, and I will sorely miss doing that.

# Prosthesis Fitting

## Thursday, 12 May 2016

Today was my prosthesis fitting appointment. I went with a friend instead of Gus because I thought this was at least something I could do without him. It was strange because the first thing the lady asked me was if I had a supportive partner. I assured her I did, and she went on to describe how some men are negative towards a prosthesis, and are judgemental of how their partners look. I was shocked – how could someone be like that, knowing what their wife or partner had been through to lose a breast in the first place?

It made me think how very lucky I am to have a husband who has supported me throughout this process. In fact, he's supported me through everything since we've been together. Anything I've wanted to do, he's always been there for me including changing my career and having to study 2 nights a week at university when the girls were quite small. He would come home from a day's work and just take over with the family – he'd feed them, entertain them, bath them and get them to bed, while I went off to study. There has never been one thing he hasn't supported and encouraged me to do. I'm blessed, and it's taken this awful life event for me to truly understand what I have.

The fitting went well and was very positive. It'll take me a while to get used to as it feels a bit odd at the moment. The prosthesis itself is made from moulded silicone and is shaped exactly like a breast. They come in all shapes and sizes to suit everyone. I'd never given much thought to the vast array of breast shapes and sizes. The prosthesis fits inside a pocket in the bra and then gives the illusion of a natural look. I had taken some of my own underwear for the fitting but it wasn't suitable. Apparently, it needs to be non-wired with a deep section between the breasts. I immediately thought of the Playtex Doreen bras my nan would have worn. The lady reassured me there were lots of suitable, pretty bras out there now, and I needn't worry.

I had also worn a patterned top, which wasn't good either as you can't see how the shape looks with a pattern. The lady came to the rescue with a tight T-shirt, and I could then see the definition of my bust. These little tips would have helped if I'd known. She was very kind and chatted to me for a while afterwards about her daughter's battle with lymphoma – and I thought I had problems!

I asked to speak to the breast nurse afterwards as I'm still unsure about my scar. She reassured me it all looked fine and was settling down nicely. They're all so helpful at the clinic and nothing ever seems to be too much trouble.

My appointment with the consultant the next day was cancelled. Apparently, she didn't need to see me because I was doing well. That was good, but I wanted to see her. I wanted to thank her for saving my life and giving me the chance of living to be an old lady. My next appointment with her isn't until May 2017.

I have to wait for the oncology appointment and until then, I won't know exactly what my treatment will be. There are a few things I wanted to do this year, including a charity mountain walk in Switzerland in September, but I can't commit to this or anything else until I know for certain what will be happening with me.

# Birthday Celebrations

## Sunday, 15–Wednesday, 18 May 2016

## Georgia's 18th birthday celebrations

Georgia's 18th

I cannot express the admiration and love I have for this beautiful girl. She has turned out to be everything I could have wished for – she is kind, loving, courageous, beautiful, hard-working and uplifting. She has the most gorgeous smile that lights up a room and has the ability to make other people feel at ease with her.

Her 18th birthday was something we'd all been looking forward to, and I certainly didn't want it marred by my problems. If I could have waved a magic wand to take all of this worry and angst away from her, I would do it in a heartbeat. She and her sister have coped admirably with the news, and they have done everything they can to make the journey easy for me. I don't think I have done any housework since the operation. They make me laugh and lift my spirits –

a hug is never far away when they're around. They've been absolutely outstanding and I love them with all my heart.

Back to Georgia's 18th celebrations. We had all of the family, godparents and close friends round for afternoon tea and, instead of putting myself under undue stress, we decided to book a caterer. The afternoon went swimmingly without a hitch. It was fitting to have an afternoon where the focus was on Georgia and nothing else.

Gus gave a speech without mentioning the 'c' word – it was perfect and fitting for her.

On her actual birthday we celebrated with dinner out with the two girls and Georgia's boyfriend. It was a perfect celebration for an amazing girl.

It's been good to focus on something joyous and feel normal for a while, especially as I know this probably won't last. There is a way to go, but I know it's a journey and at some point it will be a distant memory, like the pain of childbirth, which diminishes quickly with time too.

## Meltdowns and Rosettes

### Sunday, 22 May 2016

Fizz & Phoebe

Well, today was a mixture of emotions. Phoebe and Fizz did well in a dog agility show in Luton, and I had a complete meltdown in the Milton Keynes Marks and Spencer.

As Gus and I were going to support Phoebe and would be in Luton, I thought it was an ideal opportunity to do some underwear shopping. I wanted to get there early before the crowds, so we were in the store before 10:30 a.m. It was quiet, and I was able to choose some pieces from the post-surgery section. I had ordered some online, but they were too big.

I went into the fitting room and tried a bra on. I stood there looking at every angle. Did it fit okay? Was it too big? Should it look like that? I didn't know, and I didn't want to make another purchase mistake.

I'd left Gus sitting on a sofa outside the changing rooms. He must have been worried as this is what happened next: I got dressed and came out to ask one of the ladies for some assistance. The lady at the desk said it was by appointment only and that they were fully booked today. I looked over at Gus and started to cry. I remember he asked me what was wrong, and I said something along the lines of 'I've never had to do this before, I don't know what I'm doing.' It must have been awful for him because he couldn't come into the changing rooms, he just looked on.

I went back to the changing cubicle and sobbed and sobbed. I couldn't stop the tears. I felt so distraught. How was I ever going to do this?

Then, there was a gentle knock at the door and an assistant called Pauline asked if she could come in. I let her in and she just hugged me tight while I sobbed. She came armed with tissues and a drink too. She sat and talked to me about what was wrong and how long it had been since the operation. She said she was amazed that I was even thinking about buying underwear so soon. Then she said she would help me and that I wasn't to worry. She even went to reassure Gus.

She went out into the store and came back with an armful of garments, including a tight fitting T-shirt so I could see the effect of the underwear properly.

I was in there for about an hour but by the end of it she had found me three sets of underwear that fitted beautifully – there was no rush, just calmness and soothing words. Pauline was my angel that day, and I have since sent a letter to the store to express my gratitude.

The day got better as Phoebe and Fizz won a Special Award at the dog show. The two of them work like a team and I am so proud of them. Phoebe has worked so hard with her and it is all paying off now.

# Emotions and Gratitude

## Tuesday, 24 May 2016

The last few days have been a mixture of emotions and gratitude for what I actually have around me. The amount of love and support is truly amazing. I struggle because I'm usually 'the fixer' but at the moment I'm having to let others 'fix' me, physically and emotionally.

I got over the feelings of being a freak in the lingerie changing room, and I still think Pauline is an angel.

My friend Jules was over from Canada and dropped by for lunch. We haven't seen each other since she went out there about 4 years ago, so we just picked up where we left off. She was able to give me lots of reassurance as she had worked in a Leicester hospice as a counsellor for some time, and she had worked with many breast cancer patients. She made me realise that my thoughts and feelings were completely normal; that was a comfort because sometimes I think I'm going mad.

Today was also the day I got some devastating news about a wonderful work colleague's son who was killed in a car accident. I was absolutely stunned – there were no words. I have worked with my colleague for about 18 months and, though I have never met her son, I felt as if I knew all of her children and family. She is such a compassionate, warm and caring person. She talks about her family all the time and paints a picture of a very close-knit unit. It certainly put some perspective on my own situation. He was so young and full of life, and he should have had years ahead of him. He was taken too soon and, although I'm not particularly religious, I sometimes think we're meant for other purposes. Who knows? Such a sad day.

Later today, I went off to East Runton with my friend Lucy to stay in a caravan on the edge of the cliff, looking out to sea. Our mutual friend Louise moved to the coast a couple of years ago and we, together with two of our other old school mates, have visited on several occasions. There is something about the sea and the coastline that I find comforting and hypnotic at times.

East Runton May 2016

We stayed for 3 nights and did lots of walking, talking, eating and shopping. The weather was fairly kind to us, and we were able to walk for miles. Louise even got us to climb the church tower to see the views. It was beautiful once I'd overcome my fear of heights. I could see out to sea for miles as well as the whole of Cromer. It was nice to be normal and not feel like someone with a health issue.

The first night we were there, the wind howled and kept me awake. We were so close to the cliff edge that I wondered if we'd end up in the sea come morning. We didn't and went on to have a memorable few days together. It's definitely times like this that you need your friends as well as your family. I missed Gus and the girls and was in constant contact, but it was also good to kick back and smell the sea air.

# Crazy Hats

## Thursday, 26 May 2016

Crazy Hats May 2016

Today, I ventured to the coffee morning at Crazy Hats (the local breast cancer charity). I felt apprehensive about walking in but I needn't have as I was given a very warm welcome. They were celebrating the Queen's 90th birthday today and everywhere was decorated in red, white and blue. There were piles of cakes, scones, sausage rolls and copious amounts of tea.

I was able to chat with the founder, Glennis Hooper, an inspirational woman who has been clear for 15 years now. Things were very different 15 years ago, and she tells an honest account of how she was treated at work because of her diagnosis. It was because of this experience that she had the time and the determination to set up the charity. I am astounded at what she has achieved.

While I was there, I was introduced to a couple of people I already knew. One was a lady who works for the charity but used to run Slimming World classes over 15 years ago when I attended back before Phoebe was born. She has also had breast cancer but made a full recovery. The other lady was there with her mum. Both have had breast cancer. I was introduced to Lucy, a girl that was in my class at school. How bizarre! Or maybe not? If breast cancer affects one in eight women at some point in their lives, then maybe this is no coincidence. That statistic scares me – one in eight is far, far too many. The only way more research can be done to help prevent it, is through charities like Crazy Hats. They are marvellous and long may they continue.

I have decided I will try to attend as many Thursday mornings as I can and to give them as much support as possible. They are absolutely inspirational and it's so comforting to know I'm not alone in this bubble.

# Phoebe's 15th Birthday and the Muddy Run

## Saturday, 4–Sunday, 5 June 2016

Today was Phoebe's 15th birthday and the Charity Muddy Run for Cancer Research in Northampton that my old school mates were taking part in. The day started with an opening of presents and cards for Phoebe and then passed in a whirlwind.

We went over to Abington Park in Northampton and met up with Louise, Sally, Jane and their partners and families. Unfortunately, Lucy wasn't able to join us as she was still in hospital following a bad reaction to her chemotherapy. I promised to cheer twice as loud and give twice as many hugs to make sure she wasn't left out.

The girls did marvellously and ran the whole distance even though they said they wouldn't be able to. I called Lucy from halfway round the course, and she had a chat with each of us. The good news was that she was being discharged today.

It was a very emotional event, and I struggled not to cry all morning. I can't believe Lucy and I have such great mates who have done this for us. They raised over £1,300 – absolutely amazing. I love them to bits.

Muddy Run June 2016

Once the race was finished, we all went to get cleaned up and decided we'd all drive over to Oakham to visit Lucy for an hour.

It was quite a difficult afternoon for me if I'm perfectly honest. Lucy has had a bad reaction to her first chemotherapy session, and she looked absolutely knackered, bless her. I just wanted to hug her tight and make it all better. At the back of my mind, all I could think was that it may be my turn next. I don't know that for sure as my appointment with the oncologist isn't until the 6 June.

Famous Five June 2016

On the drive back, my friend Jane put her hand on my shoulder and reassured me that it wouldn't be the same for me if I needed to have chemo. She should know, she was a radiographer for years, but I still worried as Lucy looked changed by it, haunted even. I feel so desperately sad for her – she doesn't deserve this. She is such a kind-hearted, warm human being. Why, oh why, do bad things happen to good people?

We finished the day's proceedings with a slap-up Chinese at our house. It was a shame Lucy and Neal couldn't be with us, but we will do this again when we're both well enough. It lifted my spirits, and I think we ended the day at about 1 a.m.

It has been so uplifting to share a day like this with good friends, good people and reminisce about all the good times. We've talked about weekends at the coast in the future and even a holiday to Lucy and Neal's happy place, Kefalos, where we're all going to learn to windsurf. Now that will be something worth watching.

Hope and positivity are the way forward.

# Oncologist

## Monday, 6 June 2016

Today was the appointment with the oncologist, Dr Milanovich. Given what my consultant surgeon had told me after my operation, I honestly thought I was going to have to get the consultant to explain why he thought I didn't need any chemotherapy. At the time of the operation Miss Knight said she felt that I was a belt and braces kind of girl, and that if the chemotherapy was on offer, I'd take it for the reassurance it would give me.

I've had weeks to think about whether or not to have chemo, and I was convinced we were going to have to get him to give us some concrete reasons why I shouldn't have the chemotherapy, and we'd have a battle on our hands. The scenario was completely different. He went through the diagnosis, the tumour measurements, my age, fitness, general health, etc., and at the end, said he felt it was worthwhile to have the chemotherapy as it would give me that extra chance of living into old age.

This threw me. I don't know how I felt really – shocked, deflated, upset, flat? What he said made perfect sense. I never wanted to get away with not having chemo, but I thought I might have the option of not having to go through it.

He has advised 6 Cycles of FEC-T at 3 weekly intervals, so I will have 3 Cycles of FEC and then 3 Cycles of T. This will be followed up with 3 weeks of radiotherapy and then Tamoxifen will be prescribed for the next 7–10 years.

He examined me, and I had my height and weight recorded ready for the planning meeting the next day.

We asked about a family holiday to Greece we had booked for July. Dr Milanovich felt it was best to cancel this as he didn't want to hold up the treatment and would prefer me to stay in the UK.

We drove home in silence. So much to take in again.

I felt sick to the core about chemo; how would this treatment make me feel? I hate being ill, and I had recovered well from the surgery, and now I'd be given drugs that would make me poorly to ensure I stayed well in the future. It was all too much.

On top of which, the next day was going to be my first day back at work after the operations. How was I going to explain returning to work and then taking yet more time off?

My head was a mishmash of questions and uncertainties. I tossed and turned that night for the first time in ages.

I just want to be back to feeling healthy and happy.

# Chemo D Day

## Monday, 13 June 2016

I went into work this morning to have a meeting with my manager about plans for going forward. I found this quite difficult because I don't know how I'm going to feel. I could be absolutely fine, or I could be really poorly; it's so hard when you have nothing to gauge it by. I've spoken to lots of ladies over the weeks and some have spoken of being extremely tired and losing their hair, while others have extreme nausea and sickness. The thing is, everyone's journey will be different. We're all unique and react to things and situations in different ways – there is no one size fits all.

I felt better after the meeting as I was able to be completely honest. My boss put forward a few ideas, which may or may not work, but we agreed to play it by ear. She knows I'm not a sickly person and don't take time off unnecessarily, so if I don't go back she knows I'm definitely not well.

This afternoon was also my wig fitting. I chose three wigs, which will be ordered in for me, but the NHS will only provide one, so I get to choose the one I prefer. I had thought of doing something wild like ordering a vivid red bob or a rainbow Mohican, but the lady tactfully suggested I'd probably rather see someone I recognised in the mirror. She was right, so I chose three fairly close to my style and colour. It takes a few weeks for them to arrive, so I may be bald before I get one. Gus said that it was okay – he has a Brian

May wig I could borrow from a stag do earlier in the year. Great!

The important bit – I arrived early for the chemotherapy and was told to go straight up. My nurse, Linda, sat with me and Gus throughout. First, I had a cannula inserted and then I was hooked up to a saline drip. Over the next hour, I had a cocktail of drugs ported into the line – Fluorouracil, Epirubicin (which apparently makes your wee pink) and Cyclophosphamide. She told me the red one, the Epirubicin, will make me lose my hair.

I'd heard about the 'cold cap,' which could help preserve a percentage of my hair during treatment. I would have to be at the hospital an hour early and stay for 2 hours after treatment with the cap on. It is set at -5 °C and most people find the coldness excruciating. It's like the 'brain freeze' you get after eating an ice lolly too quickly. We had quite a chat about how the chemotherapy drugs are being used to kill off cells while the cap is trying to preserve cells. Actually, I'd rather be sure any microscopic demon is banished forever. My hair will grow back, it will be emotional, but it's just part of the rollercoaster ride I'm on already.

When my chemo session was done, and the drip removed, Linda gave me a bagful of drugs, injections and remedies. I have anti-sickness drugs, injections to help increase the production of white cells, mouthwashes, constipation drugs, drugs for the other extreme and steroids. I will need a medicine cabinet just for me.

We came straight home and so far so good, I feel okay, just a bit tired. I have had a light dinner, and I'm going to bed with the TV for company.

# First Cycle – Week 1

## Monday, 13–Sunday, 19 June 2016

This week has been a mixture of emotions and feelings. There have been highs and lows, tantrums, tears and laughter too.

I have felt incredibly tired at points and just had to give in and go to bed at all times of the day. This is something I've struggled with as I'm usually an 'always on the go' kind of girl. It's almost like a fatigue that sweeps over the body, sapping every drop of energy.

I have felt sick and queasy. I can only liken this to morning sickness or a hangover on a grand scale. I haven't actually been sick though, which is a blessing. I'd rather have a raging toothache than be sick – as I've said, it's one of my phobias.

I haven't eaten a lot. Everything I try tastes different and not what I'm expecting. Even oranges don't taste like oranges. I have a strange metallic taste in my mouth from time to time and was told to expect mouth ulcers as my immune system would be taking a pounding from the treatment drugs.

I've tried to do things and later regretted it. I wanted to help with the housework and changing beds this week. Georgia told me not to, but Mrs Pig-headed insisted. I paid for it by having to go to bed for the afternoon. I'm astounded at how these drugs affect the body. I have read up on it and know a bit about it all, but I wasn't prepared for the sheer fatigue it can bring on.

I've managed a couple of short walks with the dogs, which has been nice. There's nothing like a bit of fresh air to blow the cobwebs away.

I was also not prepared for the emotional upheaval it brings. I've had a few mini meltdowns, but Saturday saw a massive one. It was as if I was spoiling for a fight with someone, looking for an excuse to blow. I found the stupidest thing to have a moan about, and it ended up with me smashing a cup, throwing a bag of sweets across the floor, and upsetting Gus and Georgia. I could hear myself and see myself acting like an idiot, but I couldn't stop it – it was bizarre. I'm normally a fairly rational person, and this was totally irrational behaviour.

I felt so angry with the situation. I've never suffered any illness to speak of in life, and this seemed so cruel. I coped with losing a breast, the surgery and recovery, but this part is a whole new ball game. I'm being given drugs to help prevent the disease returning, but they're making me ill, changing my perceptions and sending my emotions on a rollercoaster.

It's true that you hurt the people closest to you in a situation like this. Gus and Georgia have tried to be supportive and helpful, and all I did was try to hurt them this morning. Afterwards, I felt so low and ashamed. They say they understand and that it was to be expected, but I'm feeling remorseful. I've always tried to be the one who holds the family together, acting like glue in the cracks. I've always felt we have a strong sense of family, love and support, and I was trying to destroy the very foundation. They have forgiven me, but I'm not sure I would have been so forgiving.

The day meandered on and things got better. I have had a trip out in the car, walked the dogs and stayed up later today. Maybe those little white blood cells are beginning to build up my defences again. One thing is for sure, during the next cycle, I may just hibernate on days 5 and 6.

# First Cycle – Week 2

## Monday, 20–Sunday, 26 June 2016

This was the week I decided to get my shoulder-length hair cut. I wanted some control before the drugs took over and I lost my hair. I have an amazing hairdresser, Claire, at the Scissor Sister in Raunds. She knew this had been a difficult decision for me, and she made it as painless as possible.

She transformed my hairstyle into a pixie cut in minutes. It was a very emotional experience, and we were both on the verge of tears, not because of the style or cut, but because of the significance of the appointment. I've never had my hair cut so short. I think my mum may have had our hair cut very short when we were toddlers. It was either because it was an extremely hot summer, or one of us had picked up nits from nursery. The thought makes me smile as we have a photo somewhere of us on a summer holiday with Mum and Dad, both of us sporting a majorly short hair do, matching shorts and hand-knitted cardigans. The 70s were just the best.

The next time I see Claire, it will be to shave off the little bit of hair I have left before I look like someone from a zombie apocalypse film.

I had an appointment with the prosthesis fitter this week as I felt unhappy with the one I'd been given. She was very good and explained that the prosthesis wasn't the problem, but rather the underwear I was wearing. Great, I've just spent a small fortune in M&S on new underwear and now she was telling me it was all unsuitable. She pointed out that the underwear I'd purchased was too big for me, and I shouldn't have bought anything padded. None of them were structured enough, and I needed to get this right if I was ever going to feel okay about losing a breast. Harsh but true. Back to the drawing board then.

I went to Crazy Hats again this week and talked to a few of the ladies about the minefield of buying a suitable bra. Good grief, no more Asda cheapies for me then. In fact, Jayne, one of the other ladies, and I decided it would be well worth a trip to London to a specialist shop. We'd get measured properly and spend a small fortune, but be happy in the way we looked and felt.

I seriously think there's a huge gap in the market here, and I've been buzzing with ideas. I would love to help other ladies purchase something functional but pretty. The last thing I want is to have to wear the kind of bra my nan used to wear, just because it's the only option. I have no idea how I'm going to go about this, but I thought I might contact the fashion department of a university to see if any of the students would consider post-surgery bras as a project. There has to be a huge market out there if one in eight women are diagnosed in a lifetime. I'm fifty-one and I don't want to walk round looking like an old lady yet. I still want pretty and feminine, but I also want functional.

Whilst at Crazy Hats this week, I took up the offer of a holistic treatment for a small donation – how lovely! I had a very relaxing facial with the therapist, and we chatted about relaxation techniques. What a privilege to have this kind of support. It's a wonderful charity, the only one of its kind in the country, and there should be more. Every one of us, no matter where we live, should have access to this kind of care.

I've felt better physically this week, and I'm not quite as tired. The queasiness has disappeared and I've got my appetite back. I have tried to listen to my body as much as possible and have taken short naps to boost my energy levels. I've walked for miles with Gus, the girls and the dogs. I've even been back to badminton and yoga this week – all a good sign.

A couple of good friends are going through chemotherapy for different cancers at the moment. Our journeys are different, but similar. It's really good to share these experiences and try to support each other. The thing is, we're all of a similar age, and all ordinarily fit and healthy. We certainly don't fit my pre-conceived idea of someone suffering from cancer. We're not sickly people with low immune systems, many of us are fit, strong, healthy, non-smokers, occasional drinkers and healthy eaters. There is no rhyme or reason.

I was amazed at the number of comments I received from the last blog post I put up. I've just tried to be honest and open about what this experience is like for me. Sometimes it's been difficult, and I haven't felt great, but there have also been positives and lots of smiles and laughter. I'm looking at it as a life experience, one that has, and still is, teaching me things about myself. I'm learning to be much less stressed about things and to enjoy the moment. I have a great network of family and friends who support me all the way, and I have very little time to sit and dwell on the negatives. I am a positive person who will always see a cup as half full. Building on the positives will get me through, and I hope in time I'll be able to give back to those who have helped me.

Georgia and Phoebe were both sitting exams this week – Georgia's all-important A levels and Phoebe's end of year exams before Year 11. They have been superbly focused, and I really hope that what we're going through as a family doesn't impact too much on their results. They certainly deserve to do well, and I'm so proud of them for continuing to put maximum effort into the work. They are amazing to me.

After reluctantly cancelling our family holiday to Kefalonia, I was really miserable. But again, everything happens for a reason. We always promised the girls we'd take them to Cornwall each year, but opted for guaranteed sunshine and hopped on a plane to the Mediterranean instead. Well, Georgia and Phoebe will be surprised to find we're going to Cornwall at the end of August for a week. It should be my Week 3 of Cycle 4 when I feel at my best.

I've been looking at doing some work from home this week, answering emails and completing some online courses I've always wanted to do, but never had time to do at work. I don't want to feel as if I've been out of the loop for too long. I intended to give myself this first Cycle off and see how each day progresses. If each Cycle is going to be similar, then maybe I can think about going into the office sometimes. I love my job, and I miss the people I work with. They're a great bunch.

It was payday this week, which I felt slightly guilty about. It's difficult for me to come to terms with having so much time off work. Until now, I've never had to ask a doctor for a sick note. The most I've ever had off sick is 3 or 4 days at a time. I needn't have felt guilty. The HR department decided to go ahead and pay me statutory sick pay again this month even though my manager has been trying to tell them I wasn't on a probationary period. That meant 2 months without full pay when I was expecting full pay. It's not great, and I have felt as if they don't see me as worthy of pay, which has got me down a bit.

I've worked in lots of places over the years, and there are always individuals who get away with being off multiple times with little or no consequence. I do have a genuine reason for not being at work (like a life-threatening disease). It's rubbish because although I'm trying not to let it worry me, of course, it does. I'm guessing it will be sorted at some point but possibly not without some sort of grievance procedure, and that's the last thing I want to do. My focus has to be to get back to full health and then return to work, fit enough to cope with the job. Maybe this is another unexpected twist in my life, and I'll end up being an underwear designer instead.

So, Week 2 is over. One more to go before it'll be time for the next cocktail to be fed into my system. Still, that'll be 1 more down and only 4 left to go, and I'm counting down the days until then.

# First Cycle – Week 3

## Monday, 27–Sunday, 3 July 2016

Week 3 already. This is the week when everything is supposed to feel back to normal, and it pretty much does. Hooray!

I have more energy. I haven't needed to take a mid-afternoon nap all week, and I've been able to meet up with friends and family and do all the normal things. I've been to badminton and yoga and even taken up dead lifting again. I was lifting 47.5 kg just before my operation, having built up from a starting weight of 15 kg when I started just after Christmas. I've begun again at a low weight and will slowly build back up again over the weeks, hopefully.

On Monday, I noticed my hair was starting to come out, and by Wednesday I was getting very distressed about it. As I washed and rinsed my hair in the shower, I could feel bits of hair in my mouth. That wasn't pleasant. I spent the rest of the day running my hands through my hair and finding strands coming out each time. I know it probably wasn't the best thing to do, but it's like having a wobbly tooth and being told to leave it alone – impossible.

By the time Gus came home from work, I was in tears. I sent a text to my hairdresser, and she asked if I could get down to the salon in 10 minutes, which is exactly what I did. Gus was halfway through cooking a culinary delight and had to leave it to take me down. I couldn't face it alone. I sat in the salon while Claire finished another client's hair. She had long, glossy blonde hair; I tried not to feel jealous. Then, it was going to be my turn, but another client arrived 15 minutes early for his appointment, so I waited until he had his hair cut too. He was banging on about how fast his hair grows and how he needs it cut every 4 weeks – I wanted to scream at him. He didn't know my situation though. Be rational, I reminded myself.

Then Georgia arrived for a bit of moral support. I sat in the chair and Claire asked if I was ready. At the last appointment, we had discussed shaving the rest of my hair off before it started to look patchy. Claire had been really supportive and told me that although it was one of the hardest cuts she ever had to do, she understood how important it was for ladies to take some control. I'd never really be ready, and I'd agonised about this decision for weeks, but with the support of my family, I knew it was time. This is my choice and I have control. I didn't want to end up looking like an extra from Dawn of the Dead. This way I have chosen to have it all shaved off. The clippers started and in minutes I was done!

Claire says I have a great head shape and bone structure, so I can carry off the Sinead O'Connor look well. I'm not convinced, but this is how it has to be for a while. We even managed to have a bit of a laugh about it all. Claire suggested I post a picture on Facebook saying I had a Britney Spears moment at the hairdressers.

Me with no hair July 2016

I ordered some underwear from Nicola Jane, a specialist post-surgery lingerie company this week. They arrived but none of them fitted properly. Jayne from Crazy Hats and I have decided to take a trip to the Nicola Jane shop in London this month, to get measured and fitted properly. We intend to spend far too much money.

Now I realise how important it is for both of us to feel like proper women, and to get our self-esteem and self-confidence back. When you have both breasts intact, it isn't something you ever give any thought to. Why would you? I'm looking forward to that trip. I don't know Jayne very well, but I think we'll become firm friends. She's been honest about the treatment she's been through. When others have been recounting some of the more gruesome details, she has brought things back to an even keel and reminded me that we're all very different and our experiences will be too.

I went to the Crazy Hats coffee morning with my dear friend Lisa this week. We have known each other for over 18 years, ever since we were newly pregnant and have remained friends ever since. We live an hour away from each other these days, but we keep in touch regularly. She was very impressed with the setup at the charity and felt that it was a huge support and benefit to the community.

While we were there this week, one of the ladies taught me several ways of tying a scarf around my head to create different looks. I'm amazed at how a simple twist here and a few beads there can turn a plain scarf into something stunning. I'm looking forward to practising my new skills. What's the worst that can happen? The scarf could fly off in the wind, leaving me bald. Having no hair isn't that bad to be honest, and I save a fortune on shampoo, conditioner and other hair products, as well as all that time drying and styling it. Every cloud and all that.

Me with Fizz July 2016

I have thought about this a lot this week as I contemplate the next Cycle starting. I liken it to having a baby for the first time. I remember finding out that I was pregnant and though it was very much planned, I was scared to death. I listened to everyone's accounts of pregnancy, labour and birth, which just made things worse. As it turned out, my pregnancy was uneventful. I didn't even know I was in labour until I was almost 7 cm dilated. Georgia was born after a 7-hour labour, and I recovered pretty quickly.

My second pregnancy was going to be a breeze, if it was like the first, but it wasn't. Then, why would it be? Phoebe was breech all the way through. I had constant heartburn, and I could never get comfortable. She was born by elective C-section, and again, I made a quick recovery. I was still the same person, but I had had two completely different experiences of pregnancy, labour and birth.

So, thinking about this, how could two people have the same experience of chemotherapy treatment? The simple answer? They couldn't. All I can hope for is that the next 5 Cycles are similar to the first one, not great, but manageable and fairly uneventful. That would be great. Only time will tell.

I heard back from the insurance company dealing with the holiday cancellations this week. They have now asked for proof that Georgia was, and is, in full-time education. Why they didn't ask for this at the beginning is anyone's guess. I explained she'd just sat her last A level exam and was waiting for the results before going off to university in the autumn. No, that wasn't good enough. I had to contact the school and ask them for a letter endorsing what I'd told the insurance company. The school was great and did this in less than 24 hours. I wonder if there will be any more stalling tactics by the insurance company – it's just another thing to deal with while trying not to get stressed.

The HR department at work have decided to uphold the fact that I was in a probationary period, regardless of what my line manager and I thought. This means the statutory sick pay for the first period of sickness stands. I am very disappointed with this on principle. I'm not sure what to do next, but I will be seeking legal advice as I feel it's a shoddy approach by a county council.

On Saturday, Gus and I went to a friend's 60th birthday barbecue. I was nervous as this was my first outing in public with people I didn't really know. I need not have worried – it was fine, and everyone complimented me on my choice of head attire.

It's been a mixture of emotions this week, mainly positive and upbeat but with a tinge of sadness. I was hurt by a flippant comment someone made without really thinking. After a good cry, I felt better; maybe I'm just being over sensitive.

I am truly blessed with the wonderful friends, family, neighbours and work colleagues I have around me. The support has been phenomenal, and I'm overwhelmed a lot of the time by how supportive they all are. I've lost contact with one or two friends since I was diagnosed, which has been hard to come to terms with. They haven't acknowledged the situation even though I am 100% certain they know what's happened. It makes me realise how special the people I do have in my life are to me. I am one lucky, lucky person to be surrounded by such special individuals.

# Second Cycle – Week 1

## Monday, 4–Sunday, 10 July 2016

Possibly the worst feelings in the world this week – I was an emotional and physical wreck. Who'd have thought that could ever happen to Debbie Paton. I've always been described as strong, robust and resilient. Well, not this week.

Phoebe went off to Barcelona on Monday at 1:30 a.m. on a school trip. We all went to see her off – it was her first time abroad without us, and she's my baby, even at 15 years old. I know she'll have a ball, but it's still tough seeing her go. She will be back on Friday, and it can't come soon enough for me.

And now for my second cycle of chemotherapy. The appointment with the registrar was pretty routine, and my blood tests were okay to proceed. The oncologist was happy with the fact that I'd been fairly okay after my first treatment and wanted to continue the treatment as planned. She asked if I was able to get up and about for more than half of the day – this surprised me! Yes, why not? The fact that I'd done so well after the first treatment and had been up and active for the majority of the day, seemed to surprise her. I had been getting up at a normal time and going to bed as usual throughout. The only thing I had done differently was to take a nap in Weeks 1 and 2 to recharge my batteries. I listened to my body and did what I thought was best.

She was also surprised I'd been out walking the dogs for miles with Gus and the girls and been back to badminton and yoga classes already. I explained that, although I know I'm poorly and need to look after myself, I also need normality to recover quickly. She seemed impressed with my approach, but I know no other way.

After a bit of a wait, my treatment proceeded. It was uneventful apart from the fact it took a while to find a vein. I think the little devils hide when they know what's coming; I can't say I blame them. One of the reasons the nurse has to feed the drugs carefully through a port is because it would burn if it touched the skin. Those veins must be pretty resilient! It's hard to comprehend how something so potentially damaging to the skin can be pumped through the veins. It makes me sick to think how poisonous the drugs really are.

My nurse was great today, and we chatted the whole way through the treatment about anything and everything, and the time passed quickly, which was great. Before we knew it, Gus and I were on our way home.

The effects of the chemotherapy kicked in the next day and boy did they dish it out this time. I have never in my life felt so low, so nauseous and ill. I just wanted to crawl under a stone. I am so used to being on the go and running around, but this week it hasn't been possible. Everything I try to eat makes me feel sick and even drinking fluids was becoming difficult. I am the sort of person who would rather have toothache than feel sick. At least a paracetamol takes the pain of toothache away. It seems nothing can make sickness better and believe me I've tried it all: ginger biscuits, peppermint oil, root ginger, etc.

It was a rollercoaster that I had to ride, and I'm not looking forward to the next trip if it's going to be the same. Everyone keeps saying 'two down', 'not long now', 'a third of the way there.' I know they mean well and are hoping to spur me on, but I feel like it's a million miles to the end of my treatment. I felt so low this week that I started dwelling on the 'what ifs,' which hasn't been good. I guess it's a journey everyone takes and it will start to get better, eventually. The trouble is, once you look your own mortality in the face, it's scary. I know we all have to die sometime, but I was hoping mine would be peaceful, in my sleep when I'm about 102 years old.

Georgia went away on holiday on Wednesday with her boyfriend. This is her first time abroad without us. She's a good girl and very sensible, but I can't help worrying about her. Gus took them to the airport because I wasn't up to it. He got caught up in a diversion off the M1 and it took him 3 hours to get home.

I tracked Georgia's flight to Kefalonia and cried when it landed. Silly me, I did the same with Phoebe's flight earlier in the week. Of all the thousands of flights a day, why would there be a problem? But equally, in my head, there would never have been an illness in this family. Look at me now. Unexpected things happen no matter how hard we pray they won't.

It's been a tough old week all round. These drugs have definitely hit me harder even though they're exactly the same as the last time. I wonder if there's a build up of them in the body and each time it will hit me a little harder? Maybe my immune system isn't as chipper as it was at the start of treatment, and emotionally, I haven't been in a good place.

Georgia had a difficult time settling in in Kefalonia even though she's in a familiar place, with people she knows well. She got upset and wanted to come home, but luckily her boyfriend is understanding and helped her through. I feel so guilty because she should be having a fab holiday and not worrying about me. This bastard disease, it takes so much away.

All in all, it has been a pretty tough old time. We should have been in Portugal for a few days while the girls were away, and of course that didn't happen. We were so looking forward to spending some time together, just the two of us, like the old days.

It's been 24 years since we first met at a Summer Ball on 4 July in Simpson Barracks, Northampton. I only got invited because one of my girlfriends did the table decorations and was given two tickets. She didn't have a partner at the time, so she invited me. Fateful night as Gus was only over from Germany because he was competing in the Army shooting team. I always believe some things are just meant to be, and this meeting was destined to happen.

Night I met Gus July 1992

I remember, years before, after my first marriage failed after 19 months, I went to see a lady who read my cards. She said I would marry again but not for some years, and she was right. She also said I'd marry a man from overseas but that he wouldn't necessarily be foreign. That meant absolutely nothing to me at the time, but she was right again. He was stationed overseas, but Gus was born in Oxford and raised in Lancashire.

Our wedding April 1993

I was supposed to be going to the 80s Flashback concert in Rockingham for the weekend with my mate Karen, but of course that didn't happen either. I was gutted. We'd spent so long talking and planning that weekend. It transpired I'd booked the tickets on 31 March, the day before I was diagnosed.

I've found myself feeling envious, and I'm not usually a jealous person, but everyone seems to either be away for the weekend, at a concert, having a picnic, or on holiday all over the world. I guess it's like when you're a teenager and break up with your boyfriend, every song on the radio is personally directed at you, or so it seems. Clearly, all of this is irrational thinking. There must be people in my predicament who feel the same way about the pictures I post. Pictures of us from all over the place, holidaying, eating out and enjoying life!

Again, I am overwhelmed by my friends' and family's generosity and support this week. They have all got me through, and I hope one day I'll be able to repay each of them in some way.

Right, time to put my big girl knickers on and face this thing head on. Today begins Week 2, and I've been feeling so much better over the last 24 hours. Long may the recovery continue.

Time passes and so will this.

## Second Cycle – Week 2

### Monday, 11–Sunday, 17 July 2016

This week has been so, so much better. The nausea has disappeared, and I'm feeling more myself. I haven't even had that many naps during the day this week, which I presume is a good sign.

The best news of the week was Georgia arriving home from Kefalonia. Now I have both my girls home, and I feel so much better emotionally. I never realised how much they add to my strength. As a mother, I've always felt it my job to provide emotional stability for them, as well as their dad, obviously. And he is the rock that never waivers. But the last few months have taught me this is a two-way process now that they are older. They give me as much as I give them these days, and when they aren't around, frankly, I am a bit lost. I believe that's partially why my second dose of chemo affected me more, not so much the physical side effects, but definitely the psychological ones.

As with Phoebe's return from Barcelona last week, I tracked Georgia's flight home. She texted me right up to the moment the plane was about to take off, and I spent the next three and a half hours tracking the flight online. My lovely niece, Hannah, who owns a local beauty salon, offered to paint my nails, so I left my flight tracking to go to her shop. We ended up tracking the flight while she painted my finger and toenails the colour of the Ionian Sea. We tracked it to 400 feet above the ground at East Midlands airport with a land-speed of 120 mph and 2 minutes to landing. I must have held my breath for the whole 2 minutes. The moment the screen lit up with a big tick and the word Arrived, the relief was palpable. A minute later a text from Georgia came through, 'We have landed safely.' Emotion took over and I could have sobbed like a baby.

The rest of the week has been good, a mixture of meetings with friends, family and lots more laughter.

I eventually managed to log on to my work systems and even did a few hours work. I really must have been feeling better.

I went to the Crazy Hats coffee morning again this week, but this time with Georgia, and my sister, Alison, who came along for moral support. I love this meetup, it's so refreshing to just be myself with a group of people who 'get' where I'm coming from. With the best will in the world, it is hard to understand how I'm feeling if you haven't been through it. The Crazy Hat women have either been in my position or are in it right now. I know there will be some friends for life from this gathering. I don't have to pretend to be okay, to be brave or even to be positive all the time. Here, I can say how I feel and someone will understand and offer their experiences to support me. I know once I go back to work I won't be able to attend as often, but I really hope I keep in touch with them all.

I bought a beautiful pashmina for £2.00 at the coffee morning too. What a bargain! While I was there, I took part in a relaxation session, which was needed. The therapist talked us through some relaxation techniques and then, while a visualisation tape was playing, she did some therapeutic touch, which is a very light touch of the head, neck and shoulders while you're seated. The warmth from her hands, even though she was barely touching me, was intense. I'm so glad I have access to such a wonderful service. Alison and Georgia each had a session, and as Georgia has an interview tomorrow at the local supermarket, it may help her stay calm!

Elaine, the therapist, showed her the pressure point for the solar plexus, which can be used in times of stress. It was a useful tool later on in the week when Georgia and I were trying to close a savings account at the Building Society, and it appeared we needed to jump through hoops. Oh, the other massive positive – Georgia got the job! Her discount at the Co-operative supermarket will come in handy.

The only drawback to the relaxation session was Alison. She got quite tearful at the end – she said visualisation always does that to her, but I thought I heard her say she also felt a presence in the room. Now, in the past, she's been part of a spiritualist group, and although she doesn't attend anymore, I guess she's still open to whatever is there. I didn't ask her anything more about it, but later that evening the therapist sent me a text asking whether I'd enjoyed the session and that she needed to talk to me. Well, that was the catalyst for my irrational brain to take over.

At dinner that night, I was talking to Gus about it. 'What if it was my nan or grandad coming to fetch me? What if they came to tell Alison that it would be okay? What if the presence was the Grim Reaper?' My mind was in overdrive. Gus reassured me as best he could, but it played on my mind until I eventually spoke to Elaine. It was nothing to do with what I was thinking at all. She wanted to know if my sister was my carer. I laughed and said no, I don't need a carer. Apparently, carers have access to the same services offered to the group, but others are asked to make a £10 donation for treatments. As Alison had asked for a facial next week, Elaine was just checking. Grim Reaper indeed. I really need to rein in my thoughts sometimes.

Some of the other girls at the group have included me in their quiz team for September, so I need to brush up on my general knowledge.

I went to yoga again this week, which was also very good for me. I absolutely love yoga and the benefits it has given me.

Phoebe completed her Bronze Duke of Edinburgh Award this weekend, so I am completely in awe of her at the moment. She managed to complete all the components required: volunteering, skill challenge, physical challenge and the expedition, all in the last few months. That's absolutely commendable considering what she's been up against with me.

We had a quiet weekend, walked for miles with the dogs and sat in the garden drinking cool beverages.

Gus & I July 2016

I have booked a few things for the future too: tickets to see Jools Holland and his jazz band, a weekend away in London with Gus, staying at the Tower Hotel overlooking the

Thames, and tickets to see the Carole King story, Beautiful. I can't wait.

This is the beginning of me feeling more and more positive – life is going to carry on. These drugs are being pumped into me to prevent anything returning. I will be back to full strength soon, and this will have been a mere chapter in my life, a lesson to be calmer, less stressed and to enjoy the moment. Life is for living not stressing. This is NOT going to define me, this is just ONE of the MANY things that define me.

Bring on Week 3.

# Second Cycle – Week 3

## Monday, 18–Sunday, 24 July 2016

Week 3 has arrived, and it is so much better than Week 1, that's for sure. It's strange now how I yearn for Week 3, as it's the time I look forward to the most. I have more energy and more desire to go out there and grab life by the balls.

I have packed so much into this week – it could've been a diary entry spread over a lot longer. It's been a week of busy-ness.

The week started with a trip to Animals in Need in Wellingborough with a baby sparrow. Gus found him (or her, we're not sure) on Sunday, and we think he had flown into the window and dazed himself. All day we kept him safe and tried to coax him with food and water. He made no attempt to fly or even stretch his wings, and I felt sure we'd wake up to a burial. He was alive and kicking the next morning and spreading his little wings. I contacted the shelter, and they asked us to take him over. We put him in a little basket with tissues around him and set off. He was a born traveller – no sickness or any attempt to fly off. The people at the shelter were great and put him straight into an incubator and fed him something more palatable than the diet of linseed and strawberry I had tried. I will ring to get an update later in the week, but they think he is uninjured and will be fine in a day or two. We're affectionately calling him Jack Sparrow.

Tuesday was my great adventure to 'the smoke.' I travelled down to London with Jayne from the Crazy Hat crew. We were heading for the specialist post-surgery store, Nicola Jane, in Clerkenwell. It happened to be the hottest day of the year with temperatures in the 30s. Luckily, the store was air conditioned – what a welcome that was. The ladies in the store were fantastic – professional, empathetic and full of humour too, which I need to get through these situations.

Needless to say, both Jayne and I came away with some wonderful purchases. I have four new bras; a mix of practical for work and very feminine to make me feel less of a freak. Maybe that's too strong a word to use, maybe to make me feel less 'different' would be a better way to phrase it.

We were both on a high from actually getting the service and the garments we truly needed to help our recovery. The ladies even asked us if we'd be prepared to model for them. Really?

Jayne and I had a scrummy lunch outside a pub and chatted about our lives. We didn't really know each other very well until today. Jayne told me where she worked and what she did for a career, and that a good friend of mine, Annabel, worked at the same place. Apparently, Annabel had talked to her about me, and Jayne had asked her to pass on her phone number to me if I needed to talk to someone. I actually had Jayne's number in my diary but had not got round to calling her. I firmly believe some paths are meant to cross and one way or another fate will intervene – this is a classic example.

On Wednesday, I went into work for a meeting with my manager. We discussed my issues with pay and the fact that HR are insisting I was in a probationary period when I clearly was not. It appears the only way forward is to lodge a grievance, which I don't relish doing. However, on principle, I feel it's a fight worth fighting. It's such a shame this has happened, and I hope it won't affect my relationship with my manager; I've always felt we are on the same wavelength. It's an HR issue, but it impacts all of us. We've arranged that I work from home some of the time during my better weeks and go into the office as and when I'm able to. This has taken a load off of my mind, and I feel happier about work.

On Thursday, Gus, the girls and I went to Bicester Gliding Club to watch Gus take a couple of winch gliding flights. The lady who took us across the airfield and back asked if I was having chemotherapy. She said she'd had breast cancer 5 years ago. It was quite out of the blue for her too. She hugged me tight and said I would get through it and be a better person for having gone through it all. She said she only took up gliding after her treatment and is now totally smitten. I'm not too sure about that. People say I am brave, but I don't feel as if I am. Brave is letting that elastic band fling you into the air in a plane with no engine.

Gliding June 2016

On Friday, I went to the Nene Centre for my routine blood tests. There were lots of people in the waiting room, but I had the courage to use my 'chemo pass' rather than taking a ticket and joining the queue. I could feel everyone's eyes on me with the same question, 'Why is she going in first?'

Phoebe came with me because she needed a blood test and hadn't had one before. She came in with me so she didn't have to wait in line for her number to come up. Getting to jump the queue is one of the few perks of treatment. You don't want to have to sit and wait with people who may unwittingly pass on their germs. My immune system is still low.

Saturday turned into a garden frenzy. We decided to blitz the place. I weeded and Gus power washed the patio and round the outside of the house. We were knackered at the end, but it was good to sit with a glass of wine, yes, a glass of wine (I must be feeling better) and look at what we'd achieved. I love my home.

# Third Cycle – Week 1

## Monday, 25–Sunday, 31 July 2016

Well, what can I say that hasn't already been said before? Week 1 is always going to be awful. Feeling like crap and having no energy, coupled with a low mood is enough to send anyone packing. I wish I could just check myself into a hotel overlooking the sea and order room service when I need it. All I need is the view and a few essentials. I think this would take the pressure off everyone around me too; I know I'm a complete nightmare to live with during this week. I don't feel sorry for myself, but I know I'm irritable and, to be honest, a complete bitch at times. I guess it's to be expected, but you've got to have a concrete constitution and a tin heart to be near me. Gus, the girls, my family and very close friends are the only people I want to have contact with. At least they know the real me and know this is just a phase and like everything else, it will pass.

If I could be packed off to the seaside alone for a week and picked up at the end, everyone would have a much better time of it. Enough of the whinging, time marches on and at least now I've had 3 of the 6 treatments. Yay!

Monday was D day again. We arrived at the hospital and went in to see the nurse, or so I was expecting. It turned out there were two nurses in the room and the oncologist. My heart sank. Why are all these people here? It must be bad news. My blood tests say I have something else? It's terminal. Get a grip woman. It wasn't that at all, it was just routine. Weigh me – perfect, blood tests – perfect. How do I feel? Um, okay-ish. So, time to get on with next cocktail!

As I sat with the chemo drugs hooked up to my arm, Gus and I chatted to the nurse about how she was poisoning people for a living, which we had a laugh about. I even told her how once I was so pissed off with Gus for something (can't for the life of me remember what though, but it was over 20 years ago), that to get my own back, I'd crushed laxatives and put them in his coffee. She howled with laughter, especially when Gus told her it had had absolutely no effect on him.

We left the hospital and went to pick my wig up – at last, it had arrived. I chose one from the three ordered, and the lady trimmed the fringe. I wore it home to get used to it, but I haven't had it on since. It makes me feel physically sick. I'm not sure why. It's a bit of a shock to have hair when I've grown used to being without it. I have spoken to my hairdresser, and she's going to see me next week to give it the once over, and I'll take it from there. I almost feel more uncomfortable wearing it than I do without it, if that makes any sense. Probably not.

The week progressed as usual with Tuesday through to Saturday being not great. So, no real changes in symptoms from last time, but I feel they've been slightly worse, for slightly longer. I could be wrong. I could just be getting pig-sick of feeling like poo.

I have found myself being envious of everything everyone else is doing – meals out, holidays, shopping, laughing, etc. It's all ridiculous I know. I've had all these things and will have them again, but just now it feels like that time will never come.

I had to cancel a dinner date with friends this week as I just wasn't up to it. The only exercise I've managed is a few short walks with the dogs, and I've been done in afterwards. I know I have to listen to my body and not push myself, but it's hard when that's all I've ever done.

Positives this week:

My friend Karen from work came for lunch and we laughed and cried together. Sometimes I think that's what we both need for very different reasons. She has to come to terms with never being able to see her son again after the accident, and I have to come to terms with the fact that I've had a brush with death; both very different and both very difficult.

I've spent hours and hours of my working life counselling children, adults, teenagers, trying to make them understand that you can't run away from your thoughts no matter how hard you try. Can I practice what I preach? It's damn hard.

I was paid this week and the HR department appear to have righted a few wrongs – hooray. I'm in the 'black' again! I hadn't needed to lodge a grievance. My manager worded a few good emails, and it had all been resolved.

I have booked two theatre trips to see comedians Russell Kane and Rob Beckett and a night away for Gus's birthday in November.

Gus cooked one of his delicious homemade meat and potato pies for dinner on Sunday. God, I love him.

My wonderful family and friends are still here for me even though I've been a pain in the arse.

On top of all that, I've discovered that, Leanne, the helpful girl who taught me to tie a headscarf at Crazy Hats a few weeks ago, is the daughter of a lady I worked with at the Co-op in Raunds over 12 years ago. Not only have I discovered Leanne works for the company that works in tandem with the Youth Offending Team, even spookier is that she's a good friend of my neighbour Claire, who has also had breast cancer. I am doing the flowers for Claire's wedding in a few weeks and will be at the wedding, hopefully, as will Leanne. Now if that doesn't prove that it is a very small world, I don't know what does.

Bring on Week 2 as fast as possible because then I will hopefully be feeling better.

Right now, it's the 'Sun' tarot card my sister-in-law, Lou, gave me that makes me smile. She 'drew' it for me in a reading when I was first diagnosed. It represents my future.

# Third Cycle – Week 2

## Monday, 1–Sunday, 7 August 2016

Hallelujah, an improvement in physical and psychological well-being.

Much better week, still have a bit of nausea but nothing I can't cope with. Nikki from the chemotherapy suite rang to see how I've been. She asked if I had taken any extra medication for the nausea and explained there are no medals for suffering. That made me laugh. I know there's no reward for feeling rough, but I haven't felt nauseous enough to warrant taking more medication. I actually hate taking any meds – it means I must be ill. I normally struggle to take paracetamol when I have a thumping headache, so this is a real test for me.

I'm not like this about pain, just illness I think. I know this because having given birth to two children, I can never understand why women proudly announce they've done it without any pain relief. All I ever think is, 'Are they completely mad?' Pain relief is there for just that, relief from the agony. I'm not ashamed to say I had an epidural in the end with Georgia and it made my memories of her birth good ones. Phoebe was a different kettle of fish altogether. She was a breach baby from the start and never moved – she was comfy. I was told all along that she was going to be a big baby, although, as it turned out, I'm not sure 8 lbs 10 oz was particularly big. She was born by elective C-section, but again I had a birth that was a good memory and safe for her. Bless her, I can still see her peachy little face – not a blemish.

Monday was a momentous day in the Paton household as our puppy, Dave, was off to the vet for his little operation. He was bounding around completely oblivious of what was to come. I felt quite sad for him. The operation went well. Even though he only had one visible testicle, the vet found the other one, and he was soon back home recovering, if a little sheepish. My task for the week is to keep him quiet. He's a Jack Russell. I've got no hope.

Fizz & Dave

On Tuesday, Georgia and I went to the flower wholesalers where I used to be the manager. It was quite an emotional visit for me – so many colleagues were there, and it was great to spend some time with them. I have wedding flowers to do for Claire, who was our babysitter and someone I consider a friend. She has also gone through breast cancer in the last few years, and she has only just turned thirty. She is an absolute inspiration to me, and I'm so looking forward to the wedding.

Wednesday was spent with a very good friend who's struggling with a different type of family issue. She didn't want to bring up her own problems, knowing how insignificant they would appear compared to what I'm going through. I spent some time trying to explain to her that everyone has a problem, issue, bereavement or illness to deal with at some point in their lives, and each are equally important to them and their immediate families. It makes me realise how life is a rollercoaster of emotions and happenings. None of us really knows what is around the next bend, good or bad, happy or sad. Just as well really or we'd spend the good times fretting about the bad things to come.

I watched The Bucket List this week, and it raised an interesting question: if you had the choice, would you want to know your expiry date? Well, 94% of people said no, because there are times in life when knowing something just isn't going to help at all.

Thursday was the last Crazy Hats coffee morning before the summer break. There were lots of people there today, and the atmosphere was happy and uplifting. I love this group, the people have given me so much support and hope for the future. I hope I'll be able to continue to attend now and then even when I go back to work. I would like to be there in months to come, after my treatment has ended, and to give support to people who are newly diagnosed. Dealing with the diagnosis is a scary place to be, and you can feel so isolated and alone with your own thoughts. The group is warm and nurturing; it makes me feel like I can do anything if I put my mind to it.

I have felt better and better as the days have gone on, and we've even had a couple of meals out with friends in the evening. It's good to do normal things – dressing up, putting on some makeup and getting out there with the rest of humanity. I love people, and I love engaging others in conversation. I am definitely not a loner!

My gorgeous hairdresser, Claire, at the Scissor Sister, trimmed my wig on Saturday. The fringe looked like a Dulux dog when I arrived, but she has made it look presentable. I'm not sure I'll ever wear it though, as it still makes me feel a bit sick. It's a bit creepy to me because it's not how I really look. I made her laugh even though she is a bit too young to remember this, when I said the wig reminded me of a sketch from the kids' TV programme Michael Bentine's Potty Time, where there's a wig-like creature with glasses in a sandpit (some of you of a certain age will remember that).

Claire asked if it was okay to use straighteners on the wig. I hadn't a clue, so she tested a bit she'd cut off and it melted the hair. Oh dear, it wasn't real hair as we'd thought, it's synthetic. We laughed about not leaving it near a mirror in the sunlight or it might catch fire. If I'm honest, I look forward to burning it or binning it after treatment. There is no substitute for real hair. I can't wait to have enough hair to put in a ponytail and have the feeling of it swishing as I walk. I never realised how attached I was to my long blonde hair. Hopefully, by Christmas, I'll have a covering again. It may be a while for the ponytail, but it'll happen, eventually.

Phoebe & I July 2016

On Sunday, the girls went off to spend the week with their grandparents in Lancashire. We took them to Rugby railway station, and they travelled by train to Preston. I'm going to miss them, but I know they need some time to be them. We're going to join them later in the week, so it won't be too long.

We spent the morning suit shopping for Gus, so he has something to wear for the wedding. He ended up buying the first suit he tried on even though I'd made him go and look in another half a dozen stores first. It was good to do something as simple as shopping and just blend in with the crowds.

I do notice the way people look at me; they hold their gaze a split second longer than normal, or maybe I just think they do. Now I have no hair and either wear a hat or a scarf, it draws attention to the fact that I've been poorly. Why this worries me, I'm not sure. I guess I know that when I see someone with a hat or scarf covering their head, I feel a pang of sadness for them. Ironic now I know.

I remember being in that hospital corridor waiting to go in for the results in April, and a young lady in a headscarf was sitting next to me. I wanted to give her a hug. I naively thought that would never be me, and a few minutes later I got the devastating news, and the realisation hit that I'd be just like the young lady in the waiting room.

Georgia & Phoebe Aug 2016

The huge positives this week are that:

I am almost halfway through chemotherapy. Yay!

The next cocktail of drugs, hopefully, won't be as harsh.

I have managed to do some work from home, and that makes me feel part of something again.

I have played badminton for 2 hours and been to yoga.

I will never take my friends and family for granted. One of my superb mates who lives in Wiltshire, sent flowers this week to congratulate me on being almost halfway there. It made me laugh and cry – I am so lucky.

And this is a complete saddo one. We had a tall larder fridge delivered for the garage. I'm so excited to have all that space to keep things cool – told you it's a saddo thing, but it's sometimes the little things that make a huge difference.

Looking forward to Week 3 and a few days away up north.

Me Aug 2016

# Third Cycle – Week 3

## Monday, 8–Sunday, 14 August 2016

Week 3, the week I look forward to, the week I want to do everything, go everywhere, see everyone. Live life to the full.

It's been a busy week filled with family, friends, work, new experiences and lots of reflection on life.

The girls are safely ensconced with their grandparents in Freckleton, Lancashire, having a whale of a time. They have been doing some work at Barrie's factory, Polytank, for which they've earnt some pennies for holiday money, so they're happy. They've been taken all over the place for lunches and dinners and are having a great time spending quality time with Phyllis and Barrie.

I tried to spend Monday quietly at home as I had nothing planned. I did a few hours work looking into a new acupuncture service at the Youth Offending Team, and I even started an online course in how the Youth Offending Service operates. It's interesting and something I've never found the time to do at my office desk. I blame that on Karen Jones, her yummy baking and interesting conversations.

On Tuesday, I went into work to meet up with my boss, Cath. We discussed the plan for the next few months and agreed on a few things: I won't be working during Week 1 of treatment, but I will work from home in Weeks 2 and 3 and get into the office when I can, so I don't fall out of the loop. I appreciate this level of inclusion. I know I can't push myself to do too much, but I want to feel that I'm being productive and worthwhile. I guess that's all about self-worth and self-esteem.

On Wednesday, I pushed myself and tried something I've never done before, and it was a real challenge for me. I had bought Gus a day of canoeing with Canoe2 (who are absolutely amazing, I have to say). It was for two people, so I tagged along armed with drinks, snacks, sun cream, hats and waterproofs. Our aim was to paddle from Thrapston Nine Arches to Oundle Mill, a total of 8.5 miles. Quite a feat for someone who's never set foot in a canoe.

Canoeing Aug 2016

Luckily, Gus has a lot of experience in this department, having completed the Devizes to Westminster 24-hour canoe race on several occasions with the mad Lieutenant Colonel John Starling, whilst serving in the British Army. Gus and John even beat Olympians in this race so I'm extremely proud to say I too have canoed with the best.

Canoe buddies Aug 2016

We completed the paddle and even had time for a relaxing lunch sitting by the river at the King's Head in Wadenhoe. It had been a gruelling day in parts, and it completely depleted my energy levels. Paddling, negotiating locks, hauling the craft in and out of the water, it all took its toll even with a roughty-toughty partner aboard who did most of the work. I thoroughly enjoyed the day, and we paddled past some beautiful countryside. It was so quiet and peaceful like time was standing still. We saw swans and signets (and survived getting past them, as they can be quite territorial), moorhens and chicks, loads of different dragonflies and some inquisitive cows and calves.

The weather was kind, and we had some glorious sunshine for our travels. We arrived back at the meeting point in good time and were met by a mini bus to take us back to our starting point. It was an absolutely wonderful day and one that I would thoroughly recommend. I'd love to do it again. I thinking I'd like to try sea kayaking in Kefalonia next summer. Now, there's a spirit of adventure I didn't think I had.

I slept like a baby that night and really didn't want to get up early the next day, but we had to as we were travelling north for the weekend to stay with the in-laws and meet up with the girls. We eventually set off at about 7:15 a.m. and the traffic was light. We sailed up the M6 with only a few slow points around the roadworks. On route, we had decided to call in to see some friends at Runcorn who we hadn't seen for a year.

Wendy and Gordon are very good friends of ours – I met Wendy over 25 years ago when I was studying at college in Wiltshire for my floristry exams. I worked part-time at one of her flower shops in Bath – good times. We became firm friends and have stayed in touch ever since. Unfortunately, there has been sadness for Wendy and Gordon in the past year – Wendy's daughter, Emma, died of a brain tumour in July 2015. She was only 44. Emma was the life and soul of the party. Gus and I always used to joke with her that she could drink him under the table. She was quick-witted with a sharp tongue and a kind heart. All in all, she was a smashing girl. Emma has left a big hole in Wendy's heart and two wonderful granddaughters – Molly, aged 10, and Lily, aged 4. Lily is living with her father, but Molly is living with Wendy and Gordon. I'm in total awe of their energy to do this in their 70s. Molly is delightful and very mature for her years, as I discovered when the dolly sticker books I gave her didn't go down a storm. So I told her to give them to Lily and left her money to get more appropriate books. I am so out of touch.

It was a very emotional few hours – we laughed and cried and hugged. Life deals some rubbish cards at times, but with strength and support we can pull through. Humans can be so resilient when they have to be. Emma was Wendy's only daughter, so this seems such a cruel blow. I didn't know until today that Gordon also lost a child many years ago in a tragic car accident. The things we don't know about each other, eh? I often think if we had T-shirts that stated our sad and happy times, we might all be a bit kinder to one another. No one has a perfect life, do they?

After that emotional stop-off we trundled back up the M6 to Freckleton to spend the weekend with family.

It was a fantastic weekend. We were thoroughly spoilt and got to spend lots of time with some of the best people. My mother-in-law and Barrie are good people and can't do enough for us. I'm sure I will have put on at least half a stone. We got to see Gus's dad, his partner and her daughter, Kev and Lou (sister and brother-in-law), his Auntie Margaret and cousins Mandy and Nicola.

A packed few days with trips to the 40s weekend in Lytham, and a family meal out to No 88, our favourite Chinese, as well as pub meals and a wonderful barbecue with shelter in Phyllis and Barrie's breeze house (a small thatched hut used mainly in warmer climates) in the garden. A perfect few days away charged up the batteries ready for round 4 on Monday.

It was sad to leave on Sunday and I got a bit tearful, which I never normally do. I think it's the realisation that this pleasure can be taken away from any of us at any time. We just don't know if or when it will happen.

I've reflected on a few things this week when I've been alone with my thoughts, either at home or travelling in the car.

I had my teeth straightened a couple of years ago and had to wear braces for over a year. It cost a few quid, but it was my choice to do. Everyone else couldn't understand why they needed doing. The simple fact is, they didn't need doing. It was about how I felt, my self-confidence and self-esteem. It was my choice. Cancer doesn't give you that choice – I had to lose my breast. The follow-up treatment meant I inevitably lost my hair and had to put up with the other side effects to get well. It's a strange thing to contemplate, but the braces on my teeth were all about my own vanity and choice; breast cancer took those choices away. In my view, if I wanted to live, I had to lose a few things. This is no longer about vanity, self-confidence and self-esteem – it's about LIVING.

I also gave some thought to my sister Alison. She was born with a port-wine birth mark across her eye and into her head. At the time, that must have been devastating for my parents. I don't remember as I was only 20 months old, and I just accepted the way she looked. I guess Alison did too until the cruelty of other kids came into play once she went to school. I never really understood the gravity of this for her, though I did fight off some of the bullies and cruel comments in primary school. No matter how much you argue and fight with your siblings, you will always guard them with your life.

It makes me realise how she also had no choice, how she had to learn to live with the disfigurement. I remember when she entered the Carnival Queen competition in the town we grew up in, and won. I was so proud of her. As she got older, she trained as a beauty therapist and hairdresser. This stood her in good stead for life, and she learnt to apply special makeup and even had laser treatment. It looks amazing now. But my point is, she didn't have a choice, she just had to get on with it, and she did. Good for her.

The A14 to Kettering reminds me of the hospital and the reasons I'm travelling there. I hope one day I'll revert back to thinking it's the route to the cinema, or to work or the shops, rather than the route to operations, results, scans and chemotherapy. I'm sure it will in time.

It also made me reflect on other roads that bring up emotions for me, like the A45 between the Wilby roundabout and the Earls Barton turn off. I lost a dear childhood friend to a tragic accident there in December 1997. Anita Chakraborty was one of my best friends from school. That night she'd stopped during a snow storm to help another driver involved in an accident, she was an angel like that, when a van hit her, killing her and her unborn baby boy. I was pregnant with Georgia at the time, and I remember how much it affected me.

We'd only just got back in touch after a few years doing other things. I had contacted her 8 weeks earlier when I heard she lost her dear mum (I still believe her mum couldn't go without her, and she needed her more than anyone else). I received a Christmas card from her the day after she died. I still have it and always will, it's a treasure. I think about her a lot, and every time I drive this stretch of road I am reminded of how fragile life is.

A few years after I lost Anita, I had an accident on this road and during the split seconds of that impact, I thought I was about to join her. But it wasn't my time, and I survived it. Maybe she was there watching over me? Rest in peace Anita with your gorgeous baby son. You were clearly meant for better things.

All in all, this week has been incredibly busy and thoughtful, but I have lots to be positive about. Here they are:

I have challenged myself to get in a canoe and paddle for 8.5 miles.

I have caught up with some of my super mates.

I have received some beautiful flowers, cards and messages to keep me uplifted – thank you all.

I have had a great weekend away and recharged my batteries.

I have spent a few hours at the office and had a lengthy catch up with missed colleagues.

My energy levels have been great.

I braved going out without a scarf or a hat, nakedly bald. It was okay. I'm used to it now, and it's hard to see myself in a wig.

I love living, and I am nowhere near ready to give up yet. There's too much to do, people to meet, places to see and time to enjoy what is right in front of me every day. My gorgeous husband, my rock, my port in a storm, never faltering, always steady. My beautiful girls, so resilient, cheerful and joyful to be around, always. And all my family and wonderful, wonderful friends. They were always there, but I never appreciated how much they meant to me until now. I will never forget these new feelings, ever.

Bring on the next cycle – I am READY for you now.

# Fourth Cycle – Week 1

## Monday, 15–Sunday, 21 August 2016

So, this is where I officially got to the halfway point. From here onwards, I'm closer to the end of chemotherapy than the start. I'm trying to look for a positive in absolutely everything.

I had to get to the hospital early this morning to have my routine blood test in time for the 11:30 a.m. appointment. It worked like clockwork. The staff are discreet at handing out the coloured cards with a number on, and I didn't get caught up with the rest of the general public who are there for tests.

I usually have this test done on a Friday, but because we were away, I was advised to get it done this morning. I was surprised when I was shown the results later in the morning – my blood count was up. What a difference a few days can make. The body is a pretty amazing machine, even against the odds, it will fight back.

My nurse today was Naomi, the same as last time. She explained the procedure and the side effects as this was a new drug cocktail. I'll have this drug for 3 cycles and then I'll be finished with that part of my treatment. She reminded me that I'm on the home straight, and I know it's true, but it seems endless to me. I'm longing for the day when I can look back and realise how I've forgotten aspects of the treatment and how I've stopped bringing it up in conversation.

She told me she was going to hang around for a few minutes just in case I had an allergic reaction to the drug. Some people's faces flush bright red, and they can feel short of breath for the first 5 minutes. Jesus, that scared me. Luckily, I wasn't one of those people. I watched the clock tick by, and an hour later I was done. Gus and I had managed to while away the time by playing a computer word game and chatting to the WRVS lady serving teas and sandwiches. One thing is for certain, I am always well looked after there. I can't find anything to complain about, apart from actually having to be there in the first place of course. If I could change that in a heartbeat, I would.

Tuesday and Wednesday were pretty uneventful, and I managed to prepare myself for later in the week. I had a delivery from the flower wholesaler early on Wednesday morning and, with the help of my sister, got all the flowers conditioned and into water for a drink, ready for the wedding at the end of the week. I had a friend round for coffee and I felt well. This was nothing like the FEC cocktail I was used to.

Thursday was the day things began to change.

Thursday was a busy day for me as I was preparing all the flowers for Claire's wedding. I was in my element, I absolutely love working with flowers and it gives me great joy to be preparing them for a lady who has suffered with this awful disease herself and has come out the other side still smiling. It was an emotional day in lots of respects, and I was nervous because I wanted the flowers to be perfect for her. Ordinarily, I wouldn't worry too much about making wedding bouquets but these were special. I've got over 35 years' experience, so I know what I am doing, I think.

Claire's wedding flowers Aug 2016

It made me reflect on how things turn out in your working life. How did I go from florist to counsellor?

I started as a Saturday girl for a local florist in Rushden (Jan's Floral Boutique), and I was 'bitten' immediately. I was so lucky to have a teacher like Jan. She let me attempt everything and was patient enough to put right my mistakes. She taught me every aspect of a florist's day from the mundane cleaning rota of vases and buckets, to the intricate wiring of delicate flowers. It was her belief in me that spurred me on to open a shop of my own. In 1984, I won the North-East Finalist 'Make it in Business Award' sponsored by the Co-op and Shell, at the age of 19. I had the shop for a few years before I decided I needed to go to college and get some qualifications in floristry. Jan had taught me all she knew, but I had nothing on paper.

So, at the grand old age of 25, I went back to college and got those qualifications under my belt. That opened new doors for me and over the next 10 years or so, I worked for other reputable florists in Wellingborough (Glennis and Lisa Florist) and Bath (Coates Florist). My passion was in teaching and, after I completed another course to enable me to do so, I taught at Merrist Wood College in Guildford, West Oxon College and Moulton College as a floristry lecturer. I thoroughly enjoyed every minute of it. Watching a student learn, progress and accomplish something is one of the best feelings in the world. Some of my students won awards at the Chelsea Flower Show and the prestigious Society of Floristry Awards, such proud moments for me.

So how did I change tack?

Well, after my second daughter, Phoebe, was born, and I had some time to sit and think about what was next, I saw an advert for a short course in counselling at Tresham in Kettering. This was the second time in my life I was going to be 'bitten' by something. I couldn't get enough of it and went on to study for an advanced Diploma and to degree level with the University of Leicester.

When I first started training, I always said there were two groups of people I would not be able to work with: drug and alcohol clients and sex offenders. First job out of training? Have a guess – Drug and Alcohol Service. I never looked back. For 10 years, I loved working in this field. It was only when I was TUPE-d (this happens when tenders are put in, and a different company to the one you are working for wins the tender over to a corporate company), that my love for it started to diminish. No longer did I feel that the client was important, and that statistics were the way forward. Not my bag, I'm afraid.

I left and went to work as the General Manager at the local flower wholesalers (Van VLIET Flower Group) for 7 months, which was more than enough – how that didn't kill me off I will never know. Early morning starts, late finishes, weekends, no time to concentrate on the family – I hated that. When I started, the workforce of twenty-six were quite hostile towards me, but by the time I left, I had at least twenty friends. Some of them still contact me to see how I am; that's loyalty for you. I sometimes think about that time and the amount of stress I was under. Could that have been when all this rubbish started in my body? Who knows.

I took a couple of months off to recuperate because I was pretty knackered and broken when I left. It felt as though I'd failed in a way, even though I knew for my own sanity and the good of my family, I had to leave.

In January 2015, quite out of the blue, I had a call from a company that had seen my CV on a website somewhere, and they wanted to interview me. I have been one of the Substance Misuse Workers for the Youth Offending Service in Kettering ever since. Yes, it's challenging sometimes, like trying to herd cats, but I love it and love the people I work with. I enjoy the challenges that face teenagers in the 21st century. We were all teenagers once.

I digressed there I know, but I thought it might be useful to know how I ended up doing the wedding flowers for my neighbour!

The side effects started to kick in late Thursday and into Friday. I felt as if I'd been hit by a bus as every joint in my body ached and nothing took the pain away, not paracetamol or ibuprofen, not a warm bath, nothing.

We went to the wedding and stayed until the evening reception was due to start, but I knew I'd overdone it. I felt absolutely drained. We were supposed to be going to another evening wedding reception later, but I was just too tired. I felt guilty as I know our friends were hoping to see us. I purposely hadn't sent their wedding card so we would go, but it wasn't to be. With a heavy heart I put the card in the post. I just hope they had a wonderful wedding too.

On Saturday and Sunday, I tried to rest as much as I could and the aches eased a bit. Our family, and a neighbour's family, hired a narrow boat for the day on Sunday. We set off at about 9:30 a.m. and got home around 6:30 p.m. It was a relaxing day apart from the locks (not that I did too much of that work). I knew I didn't feel myself before we left, but I just hoped I'd improve as the day went on. Unfortunately, I didn't and, at one point, I had to have a lie down in the boat for an hour or so. I was so looking forward to this trip and had been looking forward to a glass of wine as we cruised along. I couldn't even face that. I hope we'll be able to repeat this trip one day when I'm feeling more chipper.

Narrowboat day Aug 2016

I went to bed as soon as we got home on Sunday because my stomach was turning somersaults. I hate the dreaded sickness and tummy upsets that come with these drugs. It's so hard to get my head around the fact that they're being given to me to make me better.

I think I placed too much faith in what everyone else had reported about this cocktail of drugs. Maybe I only chose to remember the good bits. I held onto the fact that they were supposed to not make me feel so sick. Wrong. I'm hoping Week 2 will see an improvement.

# Fourth Cycle – Week 2

## Monday, 22–Sunday, 28 August 2016

This cocktail is determined to take its toll. I've had to cancel seeing a couple of work colleagues this week and have struggled to do much work from home as planned.

Monday, today, was possibly my worst day. I got up early as I was supposed to be driving Georgia and her boyfriend, Charly, to the train station in Bedford. They were going off to Brighton for a couple of days. I practically hauled myself down the stairs, and at the bottom I felt like my batteries were completely drained. How can that be? I've always tried to keep myself fit and healthy and now I can't even manage going down the stairs. I was so upset. Luckily, my niece, Hannah, saved the day, and she arrived 20 minutes later to take them to Bedford. It took me the next 20 minutes to muster the energy to climb back up the stairs. I only got out of bed all day to use the loo.

My sister came round at lunchtime and insisted that I ate. I knew it was futile because everything, without being too graphic, exited as fast as it entered. I can see the funny side of this now but, at the time, it was no laughing matter. I hardly ever suffer from upset tummies, but this was an upset tummy to end all upset tummies. She made me a boiled egg and toasty soldiers, and 20 minutes later they came marching out again.

I spent the rest of the day just lying in bed. I couldn't even be bothered to watch the TV or read a book. Gus came home from work, and he and Phoebe insisted I ate something too – not again. I asked for a few oven chips and a pot of mayonnaise. I munched the lot and guess what? Yes, 20 minutes later it reappeared.

I was supposed to have been going to the cinema with a friend tonight, but I had to cancel. I couldn't imagine being caught short in the middle of the film.

Tuesday and Wednesday saw a slight improvement, but I was still confined to home. My tummy wasn't settling, and I was beginning to think that our plans to go to Cornwall at the end of the week would be thwarted. I even talked to Gus about going with the girls on his own, and that I'd drive down if I felt better. Of course, this was met with complete dismissal. There was no way he was leaving me in this state. This made me very tearful. I knew what he was saying, but the last thing I wanted to do was ruin their holiday again. We have already had to cancel a family holiday and a short break away for the two of us, surely not this one too. To add insult to injury, today the washing machine decided to give up the ghost on me – what great timing. With all the tummy issues there was more washing than normal!

Even through these few days, I have managed to smile a bit. I have had Phoebe here, and my sister and parents have popped in during the day to check up on me. I had to cancel a catch-up coffee with two other friends from work, but they are always so understanding. We can do it another time, but I hate letting people down at the last minute, and I seem to have had to do that so much lately. I can never guarantee how I'm going to feel.

I took my mind off feeling like rubbish by helping my mum order invitations for her and my dad's 80th birthday afternoon tea party at the end of the month. In fact, if all goes to plan, it will be the day before my last cycle of chemotherapy – hooray! Wednesday actually saw a turning point and the tummy upset began to get better. I was still wary of what I was eating but felt I was more in control, at last.

We've decided to go ahead with the holiday and will come back early if necessary.

We had dinner together this evening, just the four of us, as Georgia wanted to talk about her exam results and her decision about university. We have both tried to guide her and give her advice, but we didn't want to make the decision for her. We both felt that now she's eighteen, she needed to decide for herself. She did incredibly well with her results, and I think it was a shock for her. I think she'd resigned herself to taking up her university insurance place at Northampton, but she got into her first choice, Nottingham Trent, and was genuinely taken aback.

She decided to defer for a year and look for full-time work. She wants to get some experience in a solicitor's office if she can, even as a volunteer. She gave all her reasons for this decision and, though some were based around my illness, these were not all of the reasons, which made me feel easier about it. The last thing I want is for her to give up her dream for me. She is such a sensible, organised young lady, and I am so overwhelmingly proud of the way she has turned out.

After she made this momentous decision, the three of us each wrote on a piece of paper what we had hoped her decision would be. Phoebe thought she should go to university now, but Gus and I had said not. Secretly, for me, I didn't want her to be gone by the end of September. Some of my reasons are perhaps a bit selfish, but my main concern was that she would push herself to go and then drop out after a few months because she hadn't been ready for the huge change. She has had to cope with enough changes this year already, and that is all my fault. I totally respect her decision, and it was as if a cloud had been lifted from her once she'd made it. September 2017 will soon roll around. She made me smile so much when she said one of her reasons for staying was that she wanted to help Phoebe through her GCSEs next summer, and if she went to university now, she wouldn't be around to do that. I love her selfless attitude.

With the doggies safely ensconced at the dog sitters in Great Harrowden, we set off on our journey. We had pre-booked a hotel in Taunton to break up the journey to Fowey so it wasn't such an epic drive.

On the way down, we took the scenic route and called in to see our dear friends Paula and Stuart, in Chippenham, for a cuppa and a slice of her fresh-out-of-the-oven banana and chocolate bread – yummy. Amazingly, that snack stayed put. It was great to see Paula and the girls (poor Stuart was slaving away at work, yeah right). We had an hour or so with them catching up on news. Their two girls are similar in age to ours, so it was all about exam results, etc. It's such an intense time for them all.

We beetled off down to Taunton, stopping at Glastonbury as I wanted to climb the Tor with the girls and Gus. I had been there loads of times in my twenties, but this was the first time with Gus and the girls. It had changed. So disappointing. Now you have to get a minibus up to the Tor walk, and you can't park nearby and just do it yourself. Too touristy for my liking! Even the shops in the town were too commercialised for my taste. Their prices were high and there was nowhere particularly nice to eat. Never mind, we could see the Tor from the car park, so that was enough mystical stuff to end the day.

We stayed overnight at the Premier Inn at Taunton – basic, but clean and a comfy bed. What more do you need? The tummy upset seems to have settled, and I am feeling more like my old self at last.

The next day we travelled on to Fowey. It was a bit of a nightmare journey as there had been an accident on the A38 (a single carriageway), that had blocked the whole road. I was driving and happily following the Satnav until the last mile or so, when it turned me onto a single-track road with no room to pass, except the odd dip in the hedge. The last 500 yards were the worst as we had turned down an extremely steep single-track hill, heading towards the water! I thought we were in the wrong place, but no. What a worthwhile journey it had been. The cottage was set right on the river estuary overlooking Fowey and all the sailing boats. It was a view to die for.

Fowey 2016

We had arrived early, so we went back up the single-track road and round to the village of Boddinick where we found The Ferryboat Inn. What an idyllic way to spend lunchtime, overlooking the estuary and watching the world go by.

The cottage was beautiful, old fashioned, but with every amenity needed for a perfect stay. It even had its own pontoon where we could moor a boat if we wanted to hire one. The only drawback was its seclusion. There were other cottages around us, mostly holiday lets, so there were other folk around, but if we needed anything, it was a drive out. The nearest proper supermarket was in Liskeard, some 15 miles away. We decided to bite the bullet and do this before we settled in. So, we returned from Morrisons with enough provisions to keep us going for the week. We cooked a meal and sat out on the veranda with a glass of wine and watched the sailing boats come and go and the Boddinick ferry toing and froing from Fowey.

On Saturday, we decided to explore on foot. I had briefly read the directions that would take us via a public footpath to the ferry in Boddinick so we could cross over to Fowey. Unfortunately, I forgot the directions, and we missed one vital turning by a house because it looked like their driveway. So we walked about two or three miles out of our way. Never mind, it was a beautiful walk, nonetheless. It just meant that on the way home we did it in half the time. We crossed over on the ferry to Fowey and fell in love with the place. I would definitely holiday in this area again. It's busy but not overcrowded. The views are stunning. The shops are quaint, and there are plenty of hostelries and tea shops to rest. We stayed in again and had dinner looking at our beautiful view.

I slept like a log. All of my awful symptoms from earlier in the week had disappeared.

Sunday was a bit of a cloudy day, so we decided to go on a road trip to find the sun, which we did. We visited St Mawes and Mevagissey. St Mawes was beautiful with a wide, wide bay and spectacular views. Mevagissey we weren't so keen on because it was heaving with people, not my idyllic Cornish fishing village – it's probably better out of season.

So, the week started off in not such a good place, but it ended well. I was in a beautiful part of the country with my family close to me. It's been a long time since we holidayed in England. Somehow it seemed easier to hop on a plane for guaranteed sun, but Cornwall has surpassed itself so far – good weather, stunning scenery, friendly locals, fantastic accommodation (there was even a cream tea waiting for us in the cottage) and a whole week to enjoy whatever else we choose to do. The positives will always outweigh the negatives.

# Fourth Cycle – Week 3

## Monday, 29 August–Sunday, 4 September 2016

## A Cornish treat

This week has been fantastic, a real positive in my journey. Gus and I hadn't been to Cornwall for 20 years and the girls had never been. It has been everything I hoped for. The accommodation was perfect and in such an idyllic setting, so tranquil and picturesque, like a setting from a Daphne du Maurier novel. In fact, a home she lived in was across the water from us.

Spending a whole week with Gus and the girls has been welcome too. For the past few months, there have been lots of visitors, and it has sometimes been difficult to devote enough time to the really important people in my life. I hope that doesn't sound ungrateful, it's not meant to. I've been overwhelmed by the support from family and friends, and I joked with Gus that he'd have to book a big venue if I snuff it!

What this week has enabled me to do is chill out and give my time and attention to the three others in this family unit. It's easy to lose sight of the fact that they've also been on a journey, and one they wouldn't have chosen to take either. Since April, the Patons have been on a rollercoaster of life and still had to perform normal, everyday tasks as well as cope with work and exam pressures and university callings. This time together, without any interruptions, has given us the time to talk to each other, time to express all of our fears and consolidate. We are a strong unit, and for that I will always be grateful. I consider myself one of the lucky ones,

I've got a partner and children who will stand by my side through the good and the bad.

So, this is our Cornish sojourn.

Monday was a packed day with visits to Polperro, Looe and Polruan as well as a vintage steam rally at Morval. The steam rally took me back to a time when my parents would take my sister and I off to the Peterborough Expo each year. The smell of the smoky engines mingled with candy floss and Cornish pasties, a real nostalgic treat. There were vintage cars, traction engines and Gus's favourites, the military vehicles. He was particularly in love with the 'Green Goddess.' It took him back to his time as a teenage soldier during the fire strike in 1977.

He was actually stationed at the Territorial Army offices in Wellingborough, opposite the United Reformed Church, where we were married in 1993. I often think how spooky that is. I guess he wouldn't have even noticed me if I'd been walking past as a 12-year-old with my parents! He would have been 19 at the time. It's odd to think that our paths may have crossed then, but it wasn't the right time to meet.

Lots of Cornwall is too commercialised for me now, but Polperro still has its charm and we thoroughly enjoyed meandering through the narrow lanes. There was a regatta at Polruan and the place was heaving with crowds watching street performers. It felt like going back in time.

Tuesday was another long road trip: Tintagel to see the castle and soak up the mystical King Arthur story, Port Isaac (no Doc Martin in sight), Padstow, Watergate Bay and Newquay.

Everywhere was busy today, and I've noticed how things have changed over the years, things that were free to go and see, now charge, and have been taken over by English Heritage. I guess things need to be protected, but some of the fun of climbing over rocks has gone when it all seems to have been commercialised. Padstow was always such a beautiful little fishing village, but it's completely mobbed with tourists (okay, okay, I know I was one of them), and it has lost its charm for me. Twenty years ago, Gus and I stayed at the Watergate Bay hotel with our dog, Ziggy. We used to walk for miles on that beach. The hotel is now a fancy boutique hotel, and the bay is wall-to-wall with would-be surfers, and not a scrap of sand to be seen. Jamie Oliver has an overpriced restaurant on the beach, and I feel it's been spoilt.

On Wednesday, we walked to the ferry at Boddinick and went over to Fowey. It's beautiful here, and I feel it's still the old Cornwall I remember. We had a tour of the offshore Life Boat for an hour, and I'm totally in awe of the work these people do. It was an amazing hour of information.

Fowey 2016

In the evening, we drove to Launceston and met up with an old school friend and her family. I hadn't seen Caroline for over 30 years even though we've never missed a Christmas or birthday card. It was a nostalgic evening, and we got to meet her husband and their three children. We reminisced about the birthday parties we had each year, Caroline's in the post office her parents owned, and mine at home with the Christmas decorations still up because it's on 3 January. We laughed about the way my dad always modified the Christmas cake for my birthday by knocking off the snowy icing peaks and replacing them with pink swirls. I was the only kid ever to have fruit cake as a birthday cake. All I ever wanted was a sponge cake!

On Thursday, we went to the Eden Project. I'm glad we went but, if I'm honest, I probably wouldn't bother returning. I'm sure it was great when it first opened, but it's looking tired these days and needs some serious updating and TLC. The Biomes are incredible and the plant life is worth seeing.

Friday was the long journey home. In total, it took us almost 8 hours due to traffic jams. That's the drawback of travelling to and from Cornwall.

Saturday – today was my sister Alison's 50th birthday, and she held a little gathering at our house. It went off okay, but I was very tired by the end of it. It's good to get extended family together to celebrate.

On Sunday, I met up with a lady that I've been messaging since she was diagnosed in July. A colleague at work asked if I would message her, and we've been in touch ever since. Today was the first time we met face to face, and we spent three hours talking non-stop. Sarah starts her 1st chemotherapy treatment tomorrow, the day I have my 5th treatment. She's scared and very apprehensive – it brought all of those feelings back for me too. It's a tough journey, but once you're on it, you can see an end to it, too. It's hard to always be positive, but if you can be positive most of the time, I'm convinced it helps.

So, as you can see, this week has been very full on and very positive for me. Weeks like this keep me going when I'm having a bad hour, day, week. It's not all bad. There is always something to look forward to and enjoy even if it is just another Cornish cream tea.

# Fifth Cycle – Week 1

## Monday, 5–Sunday, 11 September 2016

At last, I feel like the end of this treatment is in sight. This is number 5, so just one more to go after this.

I arrived early at the hospital as I had to have a routine blood test before the treatment and took a yellow card with a number, my quick route into the pathology department. As it turned out, I was waiting for half an hour. I'm not sure what went wrong there! The idea is that I don't sit with people who are likely to pass on an infection! Never mind – it got done, and we went off for lunch until my appointment in the chemotherapy suite.

I saw a different oncologist today, the third so far. Gus actually took the mick out of him beforehand as he was wearing trousers at half-mast. He said, 'You'd have thought a consultant could afford some decent trousers.' This was before Gus realised the man was actually my oncologist for the day. Luckily, his personality out-weighed his attire.

He was a kindly man, knowledgeable, considerate, courteous and empathetic. He asked how I'd been, and I said I was okay but with a few rough patches. He encouraged me to ask as many questions as I wanted, saying there was no rush. Crikey, I've never got that at the GP surgery where I've always felt I've got to talk a million miles an hour (which most people would say I'm quite good at), and get out of the chair as soon as possible.

I asked three important questions:

Why had my two big toenails turned black and blue? Had I dropped something on them simultaneously and not remembered? Yeah right, Deb, don't be ridiculous.

Short answer: 'It's the drugs.' He asked to look at my fingernails and said I've been lucky it hasn't affected them too. I don't want that to happen. I'd bitten my nails on and off since I was a little girl and, since my diagnosis in April, it's made me feel physically sick to bite them. Work that one out? I can't. Bizarre.

Second, my tummy issues were bothering me. I'd had days of rushing to the loo as soon as I'd eaten. Nothing stayed put for long, and then it would swing the other way and I'd go for days without needing the loo but not feeling bloated. I explained it in more graphic detail, but I guess if you're reading this right after a meal, it wouldn't be wise for me to recount it all. I told him I've had dark thoughts that perhaps I have bowel cancer too. There is some history in my family although I think they were pre-cancerous cells.

Short answer: 'It's the drugs.' He smiled and said I didn't have bowel cancer. He completely understood the way my mind goes into irrational overdrive at times – why wouldn't it? I was perfectly healthy, or so I thought, until 1 April 2016.

Third, on all the correspondence my GP and I have received from the hospital, there is a histology section and within it, it says: 'Closest margin is deep posterior 10 mm.' This had been worrying me for ages, and I had not voiced my concern. I didn't know what it meant really, but in my head, I thought the worst. Did it mean the cancer had spread back towards my chest wall? Will it mean it's there now, too?

Answer: the consultant drew a sketch of a breast, which made me laugh as he said he was no artist. It showed areas of cancer cells and he explained how the surgeon makes sure he removes at least 8 mm from the edge of the farthest mutant cell. He explained that 10 mm was a positive thing, and this was the reason the surgeon had no option but to remove the whole breast. Invasive lobular cancer grows in the milk ducts and is not a concentrated mass, and therefore it is more complex to remove. It's not a lump that can be targeted first and then removed. It has to come away and then have the adjuvant treatment, which is given after initial treatment for cancer, especially to suppress secondary tumour formation.

I felt so much better after talking with him because he put my mind at rest about a lot of things. Chemotherapy plays havoc with your reasoning. Ordinarily, I wouldn't be as observant about slight changes in my health, but now I watch every little thing – the minutest of changes freaks me out. I hope, after the treatment, I'll return to some form of rational thought and get on with my life. It will always be at the back of my mind, but hopefully in a filing cabinet in a dusty archive room!

We were asked to sit and wait to be called upstairs. The consultant reappeared a few minutes later to say there had been an issue getting my blood results and, though he was happy to proceed with the treatment, the staff in the chemotherapy wing needed the results first. Apparently, the pathology lab said I didn't go for my blood test until 2:45 p.m. Cheeky monkeys, I was there at 12:45 p.m. and actually had my test done at 1:10 p.m. The consultant even arranged a cup of tea for us both – what a star.

After this was investigated, I was whipped upstairs only to be told they didn't have enough nurses to cover my treatment. I was feeling a bit naffed off by then. A nurse was on the phone trying to pull in another nurse from elsewhere and said if she couldn't, then I'd have to come back the next day! It's only a day, but it would put the treatment end date back further. Now my final one wouldn't be until 27 September. I didn't want that. A nurse was found, and I eventually started my treatment. We were the last people in the suite – it was 6:10 p.m. I was tired driving home, but at least it was done.

I can't quite believe how matter of fact the nurses are. It may be an everyday thing to them, but to us, as patients, and family members, it's a huge, huge deal. There were people in the unit today with three or four family members supporting them, spurring them on, willing them to do well. The human spirit never ceases to amaze me and, in times of trouble, the love, compassion and faith is so strong between us.

This second drug lulls me into a false sense of security and, for the first couple of days, I feel fairly okay. By Thursday, it begins to kick in, and it's as if I've been hit by a steam train. The best thing is to sleep and take ibuprofen and paracetamol. I haven't experienced flu before, but I'm told the symptoms are similar: bone ache, headache, slight nausea, dry mouth and the appearance of alien taste buds. I've cooked numerous meals, really looking forward to them, only to be disappointed by the taste. Now, some would say it's my rubbish cooking, but I think not. The drugs affect the taste buds and everything takes on a metallic taste for about 10 days. This will pass and, by the middle of next week, I should start to feel like my old self again.

I did go to the Crazy Hats coffee morning this week, which is a first in Week 1 of treatment, so that was a positive sign. I collected tickets for the Quiz Night on Friday, 16

September, for a group of work colleagues. It's great that they've got together a team to come and support the charity. I'm so lucky to have such wonderful people to work alongside. I'm part of a team too, called the Cheeky Girls. I bet they don't know my general knowledge is rubbish.

I've had a bit of a shock this week too, but in a good way, I hasten to add. I was looking through my emails and deleting junk mail when I noticed one from Nicola Jane, the underwear shop in London that I had visited with my friend Jayne. I read it once, twice, three times. Are they joking? We'd been asked to fill in a form at the shop and when we got home, we sent a recent photo and a brief résumé about ourselves. Jayne and I had done what was asked, but we hadn't told each other as we thought nothing would come of it. How wrong could we be?

We've both been chosen, along with four other ladies, to be part of a photo shoot for the 2017 brochure. Neither of us can quite believe it, and we're still in shock. We have to travel to Chichester for the day, and we will be photographed in two of our personal favourite bras from the new collection, then swimwear on the beach. Me? A model? That's so far from the realm of possibility in my eyes. We're both so excited though, like a pair of kids. Jayne's even told her husband that she's out of his league now. I fully intend to enjoy the experience. Who says nothing good can come out of something so bad? There is always a rainbow after a storm.

The weekend was pretty full on – the new washing machine was delivered, hooray! The little things mean so much to me these days. I had a conversation with Gus about how many things had broken in the past few months: the fridge, the microwave, the cooker, the washing machine and me. Fortunately, the white goods are easy to replace. I'm a slightly different kettle of fish.

Phoebe and Fizz took part in a dog agility show at Horton and won two rosettes. Georgia and I managed to get over to see one of her runs. I'm so proud of her – who says you can't train a Jack Russell? She's now got Dave to bring up to standard, and he is chomping at the bit to get going, but he has to be 12 months old to compete. Fizz has a posh kennel name, so when she's announced they say, 'Phoebe Paton with Matundra Fizz of the Ritz.' Dave isn't Kennel Club registered, so Phoebe has decided that when he competes, he'll be known as 'Dangerous Dave.' I can't wait to hear that over the tannoy.

Phoebe, Fizz & Dave

The weekend ended with a visit from our good friends Lisa and Graham and their two boys, James and Damon. We had a relaxing afternoon, eating lunch and chewing over life. We've known each other for over 18 years and, though we moved from the Bicester area where they still live, some 16 years ago, we have remained firm friends. We've organised a cottage over New Year in Devon, and we're all really looking forward to that as I should be feeling back to normal by then, fingers crossed.

We've even talked about a cruise holiday sometime, maybe in 2018. That would be perfect as it'll be our 25th wedding anniversary year. Planning for the future is something I now hope I have the ability to do, and I will grab it with both hands.

That conversation made me reflect on all the things we've managed to do over the years, the places we've been and the experiences we've had. The pyramids in Egypt and the museum in Cairo, the Wailing Wall in Jerusalem and the Church of the Nativity in Bethlehem when we were on honeymoon. Skiing with the girls, parasailing in Sharm-el-Sheikh, dolphin spotting in Gibraltar and the time a school of dolphins followed our boat in Kefalonia. It's endless. The memories are rich and I will always be grateful for that.

Gus said the nicest thing about his life since meeting me. He said, when he thinks of everything we've done together, his overriding memory is of sunshine and smiles. That's so good to hear, I'm so lucky. This hasn't been the greatest year so far, but it has been a good time for reflection and being thankful. I can't type anymore because I'm crying, but they are happy tears.

# Fifth Cycle – Week 2

## Monday, 12–Sunday, 18 September 2016

I purposely decided to keep this week fairly free of any engagements with friends and family as I remember this week being the worst time after the 'T' drug cycle. In fact, it wasn't as bad as last time. The symptoms were similar to before but milder, which was a blessing. I am no longer wittering on about having other problems as my digestive system hasn't taken quite such a hammering this time, and my tummy has felt more settled and normal. Hallelujah!

I had a couple of impromptu visits from friends, but on the whole, I spent the first few days of this week relaxing and pottering around on the computer with some tasks for work.

I had a nice surprise posted through the door one day (after I retrieved it from Dave's jaws as he was happily tearing the card to bits in the garden). It was a beautiful card and a voucher for myself, Georgia and Phoebe for afternoon tea when all the treatment is over. What a truly wonderful gesture. I was in tears. I still can't believe the thoughtfulness of people, and I find myself overwhelmed by it all. Gus sometimes says I should think about the way I am with friends and acquaintances and realise that I would want to do the same. I know all that, but I don't expect anything in return. It makes me reflect on my own upbringing. If there is one thing that sticks in my memory, it's that my mum always said I should treat others the way I would want to be treated. I've always followed that ethos and tried to be kind and not upset anyone intentionally. It's a good value to have, and I hope I've passed that on to my own children.

By Thursday I was feeling much better, and I went off to the Crazy Hats coffee morning with my newly diagnosed friend, Sarah. It was her first time, and she felt nervous. I was glad to go with her to ease some of her anxiety. As it turned out, she had a great time and even had her nails done while we were there. I had a reflexology session for the first time and thoroughly enjoyed it. I'm amazed at how the therapist can pick up bodily issues from points on the feet. She said that, while I was in the middle of treatment, the pressure used is lighter but recommended I book another appointment for post-treatment to get the most benefit. I will certainly be doing that.

I've had several treatments with this therapist and she is amazing. I've had an Indian head massage, back massage, a facial and taken part in a relaxation session, all of which have been fantastic and great for my wellbeing. I've always tried to make sure I have some 'me time' in life, whether that's a visit to the beautician, a yoga session or a cheeky spa day when I can. Having breast cancer has affirmed how important 'me time' is. It's an essential part of life to take some time to relax, reflect and generally be at one with the world.

In the evening, we had been invited to a presentation evening at the school for Georgia. She won two awards, one for psychology and the other for law. When the teacher read out the reasons for her getting both awards, I could have cried. What an exceptional young lady she is. She achieved fantastic results in her A level subjects despite the fact that she must have struggled to come to terms with my illness. It's as if she pushed harder to achieve. Well, it certainly paid off, kid. Gus and I are as proud as punch and can't wait for her to study Law at university, the subject she loves so much.

Friday evening was the Crazy Hats Charity Quiz night. I was part of the Cheeky Girls team and we only went and won it. I think we were all gobsmacked! We are all at various stages in our journeys and some of the team talk about 'chemo brain' and not being able to recall stuff. Well, we must have been on fire tonight. I'm not really one for quizzes, but this was an interesting evening, and although I'd told Gus I wouldn't be late, I didn't actually get back until after 11 p.m. I hope they raised lots of money for this worthwhile charity, and I'll continue to support them in the future even if I can't make every coffee morning.

On Saturday, we were up early and on the road to Cromer by 7:30 a.m. My friend Lucy and her husband had travelled down the day before. It was the 'Forties' weekend in Sheringham and the place was heaving. One of my friends, Louise, lives close by and we all met up at her house to get changed. Well, us girls did, the boys weren't so keen, the cowards! It was quite a poignant weekend for the three girls as this was the last time we could all get together before Lucy's operation on Monday. She's completed all of her treatment – having chemotherapy and radiotherapy together for weeks, and her operation is the final hurdle.

Land Army girls Sept 2016

Land Army girl

It was a fantastic weekend, and we ate, drank and danced in the street. It was tinged with sadness when Lucy and Neal left for home on Saturday evening. How could someone look so good but be suffering from something that could have taken her life? I didn't want to stop hugging her. I know she'll be okay and come through this, but it's a serious operation and she will need time to recover. Ironically, we worked out that her recovery-end and my treatment-end fall on the same date in November. How weird. We started this journey together and we will finish it together, older, wiser, healthier and with a changed view of life. 'Just grab it,' is my motto now. Just grab every opportunity and never put anything off that you could do today. You may not have tomorrow to think about it!

Lucy is in safe hands, and she has every chance of a full recovery. I can't wait to be back on the beach with her dodging the waves. As I write this, she's in the operating theatre, and I am sending every ounce of positivity her way. Come on, Lucy, hurry up and get well.

Sunday was a bit more sombre for Louise and I, thinking about our friend. We all went out for a long walk and ended up taking a wrong turning even though Louise has walked that route a thousand times. I don't think our minds were on the job today. We eventually found the right path and walked up Ingleborough Hill, which is quite a steep climb. I've decided this is my contribution to the Schilthorn Swiss Challenge that my two friends Paul and Diane are taking part in on Monday. I was due to go with them and a party of twenty, but I had to pull out due to my treatment.

I'm gutted to have missed out. I've done this walk twice over the years, and this was going to be a reunion walk for the three of us. I'm glad they've been able to take part but feel sad I haven't managed it this time. Paul is completing this challenge for Crazy Hats, so I feel especially proud. I'm looking forward to the day I'm back to full fitness and can walk as far as I used to without having to worry about how it might affect my health. It won't be long now.

We headed home in the afternoon, and our weekend was rounded off with dinner out with the girls and a trip to the Lighthouse theatre to see the comedian Rob Beckett. We had such a laugh, my sides hurt. What a funny man. As we left the theatre he shook everyone's hand, and we even got a couple of selfies with him – what a genuine guy.

Rob Beckett comedian Sept 2016

The girls had been home all weekend on their own. It's the first time that's happened without the backup of a babysitter or a family member keeping an eye on them. They were fine, and the house is spotless. Why did I worry? They're both growing up into gorgeous young ladies, and I'm so, so proud of them both.

So, into Week 3 in preparation for the last (yes, the last) poisoning session at the hospital.

# Fifth Cycle – Week 3

## Monday, 19–Sunday, 25 September 2016

This week has been a strange time for me. I've been waiting so long for this week because it means I'm almost at the end of my trips to the chemotherapy suite. But now it's here, I feel a lot of trepidation!

It's been a tough 6 months, and it's been a journey I would not wish to repeat, but it has also taught me a lot about myself that I didn't realise. Yes, I can be brave and resilient, but I can also be totally irrational and look at every little thing that could have gone wrong and still could.

I've had so many touching messages from friends, family and even from people I hardly know. It's been uplifting to know I have so much support. It has spurred me on in times of doubt. I thank you all for that and hope I'll always be as good a friend to you, if you ever need me.

This week, I've realised how often I put on a brave face and smile for the benefit of those around me. Making others feel easy around me is my way of coping. The last thing I'd want is for people to go away worrying about me and not wanting to come back because I'm a blubbering wreck. The part reserved solely for Gus and the closest of family is the sobbing and the 'what ifs?' They happen, but not often. I am only human and facing the toughest challenge of my life so far has made me look at my own mortality. I hope to live to be an old lady and die after overdoing it at an OAP party, dancing myself to death! With the great NHS service I've received, I now have a fighting chance of doing this, and I have to start to look forward to a healthy life. It's only difficult sometimes, when that little black cloud appears in my mind. I'm good at meditation and mindfulness, so I can shift these thoughts. My rock, Gus, is always there to lend a helping hand. I can move on with my life.

As this was Week 3 of the cycle, I have tried to pack in as much as possible! I have worked from home and been into the office for another meeting with my boss, Cath. She began the meeting by asking for my plan to return to work. I was a bit shocked by this and unprepared to make firm commitments. As usual, I put on my brave face, spouting that I felt good and wanted to get back to work as soon as possible. Perhaps it was the suddenness of the return that I wasn't prepared for? We loosely agreed I would return to work by 10 October. Then, after a short-phased return, I'd be back to full-time work and seeing young people by the end of the month. These plans were shared with my co-worker too, with great excitement.

It wasn't until I was driving home that the gravity hit me, and I sobbed the whole way back. Why can't I be more assertive and tell it like it really is? I won't even have finished my treatment by 10 October, and I may not even have started radiotherapy. What was I thinking? Why didn't I say 'I don't think I can do this yet'? How can I possibly see clients when I haven't got any hair on my head? It is coming back, which is great, but it's early days. What if I have a meltdown at work? I haven't had time to process what has happened to me, and I worry that one day it'll hit me, hard. How is that going to impact on work?

I managed to rationalise a lot of this with Gus when I got home. He feels it's all too soon. I have also spoken to the oncologist team, and they say 'slowly, slowly.' Their advice was not to rush anything or all the good work will be undone. They think I've coped admirably so far, and it would be silly to put myself under undue pressure. I'm not sure how to deal with this, but it's the first time I've felt stressed about having to do something. I have to be honest, but at the same time, I hate letting other people down. My co-worker has been an absolute brick, and I really don't want her to be under any more pressure than she needs to be either. It's all such a dilemma.

I recognise I have a real hang-up about admitting I have weaknesses. I want people to believe I am this strong, resilient woman who is never phased, but of course, this isn't true all of the time. I do have weaknesses, and I do still cry like a baby at The Railway Children and Love Actually.

My dear friend Lucy had her operation on Monday to remove the tumour from her lung. Unfortunately, the surgeon found some nodules on the outside of her lung that he wasn't happy with, which meant although he opened her up, he didn't remove anything. She has to wait for the results before they re-schedule the operation. I went to see her later this week – it was difficult. I feel so fortunate that my cancer was easily treated while Lucy's has been a struggle like no other. She is a positive lady though I know she has her rough times too. I hope and pray it will go according to plan for her because she's such a treasure and a selfless, thoughtful individual.

There were more positive things happening this week too. I managed to catch up with a friend I hadn't seen for ages, and I had a few lunches and dinners out so I've built myself up with plenty of calories for the next cycle on

Monday. I even had an hour's conversation with a good friend on the phone because she didn't want to come over and give me her cold before the next cycle – what a thoughtful mate.

I had to take my car to have its tyres checked at a local garage. I couldn't believe the frankness of the conversation I had with the garage owner and two of the lads who work for him. They were so open about my illness, commenting first on my hat, then asking about the type of cancer I had and the treatment. The owner kept saying, 'You're here and breathing, you're a survivor.' I'm gobsmacked at how people deal with this head on, often people I hardly know. I think there has only been one friend of mine who's made no attempt to contact me over the last 6 months. I guess I can't do much about that. Either they struggle to know how to talk about it, or they were never a true friend in the first place.

I went to Crazy Hats this week and won the raffle. Yay!

The week ended with my parents' 80th birthday afternoon tea party at our house. It went off well, and I was able to make a little speech, which made me quite emotional. It's not until you're an adult that you actually realise what a charmed upbringing you had. I think my mum and dad got the balance right and brought us up to be kind, with good morals. I hope I have passed these attributes on to my own family and that they'll look back with fondness too.

At Mum & Dad's 80th party

It was tiring for me, but I thoroughly enjoyed it. It was a privilege to have their family and friends there to celebrate with us. I can't believe they're both 80 – where does the time go? I'm lucky to still have them around and for them to be relatively fit and healthy. They've been a great support to me, too, and I don't know what I would have done without their help and devotion.

Monday is looming – my last cycle. I can't believe it. It seemed so far away when I started on 12 June, but we're nearly there.

# Sixth Cycle – Week 1

## Monday, 26 September–Sunday, 2 October

Monday, 26 September, marked the day of my mum's 80th birthday and the last cycle of my chemotherapy regime.

I felt almost wildly excited about today, a day of celebrations with Mum's birthday and the end of my trips to the chemo suite in the Centenary Wing for treatment. I couldn't wait to get there and get started. The sooner it starts, the sooner it ends. I worried quite a lot about my bloods not being up to scratch and being told I had to go back another day, but that didn't happen. My treatment went ahead as planned and I was out of the hospital in less than 2 hours. I was on some kind of high. There should be champagne corks popping and fireworks – ridiculous really, given what was actually happening, but that's how I was feeling. I knew I had an exciting couple of days ahead of me, too, and I think I was running on adrenaline.

On Tuesday, I got up and felt fine. I know this set of drugs are sneaky and they lull me into a false sense of security, but who cares, if I feel okay? I was determined nothing would stop me from doing what I had planned for the next 24 hours or so.

Today was the day Jayne and I were travelling down to Chichester for the photo shoot for Nicola Jane, the specialist post-surgery lingerie company. Excited is not a big enough word to describe how the two of us were feeling. Any thoughts of being poorly were shoved to the back of that filing cabinet in my head.

We decided to book a hotel and travel the day before as it would be a long, tiring day for us. We arrived at 7 p.m. and by the time we'd eaten, we were both shattered. We ended up sitting in bed with a cuppa, watching TV. Not exactly rock and roll, are we? Not sure we'll join the ranks of Kate Moss and Naomi Campbell.

So, the day of the photo shoot arrived. We were up early and ready to go. A chauffeur picked us up at 9 a.m. It was an amusing start to the day as both the waitress at the restaurant and the chauffeur had asked us what we were up to for the day. It's amazing the reaction you get from people when you start telling them a bit about yourself. Both embarked on stories of their own experiences of cancer with family and friends, and their own ailments. The chauffeur had suffered two heart attacks last year and had a pacemaker fitted – very reassuring when you're hurtling round the Sussex countryside at 60 mph.

Photo shoot for Nicola Jane Sept 2016

We arrived at a beautiful seaside cottage where the shoot was to take place, and from the moment the door opened, we were made to feel at ease. We had an amazing morning. I spent an hour and a half in makeup. I wondered how many products the makeup artist had to use on my face. She totally transformed me and when I looked in the mirror, I wanted to cry – I didn't look like a 'victim' anymore. It was such a wonderful feeling.

There were five of us who'd been brought together for this day, all from different walks of life and areas of the country. We were at different stages of treatment. I think the others were shocked that I was only 2 days from my last chemotherapy dose. One lady had a cold and insisted that she keep her distance to keep me safe. Only those who've been there know how vitally important this is. I know I ran the risk coming down on the train, using public areas, etc., but I'm always so careful and probably will be for some time. I know the common cold could put me in hospital, seriously ill, so I take every precaution. The one thing, other than breast cancer, that we all had in common was that none of us had modelled before! Imagine how shocked we were to discover we'd been picked from over eighty applicants! I still can't quite get my head around that.

I am an ordinary woman, I never win competitions and I would never in my wildest dreams believe that I could do this assignment, yet there I was, modelling and enjoying every moment. I have reflected since about how I see myself, and how I have viewed my body image over time. Like most women, I've never been happy with what I see in the mirror. When I was a little girl and growing into my teenage years and beyond, my mum was quite a big lady. I remember how she had a limited choice of shops where she could buy clothes in her size. Unlike today, there was no Evans or specialist sections in normal clothes shops, and she'd often resort to catalogue shopping. I remember how she couldn't run around on the beach with us like the other Mums. I remember she was unhappy with her appearance, and I remember how she tried to lose weight but always put it back on. I only ever saw her as my mum, and I loved her just as she was. It didn't enter my mind that she needed to change for her own peace of mind, self-esteem and wellbeing. My dad loved her, so what did it matter.

It was only as I got into my teenage years and understood the importance of maintaining a healthy weight that I started to look at myself. I think this had a huge influence on me as an adult, and I'm aware that I'm sometimes obsessed with what the scales say. I've always tried to keep to a healthy weight and make sure I eat a good balanced diet, as well as exercising regularly. I got more relaxed about it in my forties and became more comfortable in my own skin, but I think what has happened in the last 6 months has now given me more confidence. I would never have dreamed of modelling, let alone in my bra. My body has changed forever now and I have to accept that – today is a step on that road.

When it was my turn to be photographed, I was really nervous, but Julia the photographer was so easy-going, she made me feel comfortable. Everyone else's shots had been done in the bedrooms, but mine were done in the kitchen with everyone watching. So, there will be shots of me sitting on the kitchen work surface, gazing out into the garden, shots of me perched on a bar stool with a steaming cup of coffee, and shots of me casually rearranging the dresser, as you do in your bra and knickers. Such a laugh.

After lunch, we were taken down to the beach where we had individual shots taken in swimwear, and group shots in and around a quaint little beach hut. The sun shone, and it was just the most amazing afternoon. We all got on well and shared stories, some of which were a bit black at times, but we all understood each other. One lady, who'd had a double mastectomy, made me laugh by saying she had a boob in each pocket of her coat because she couldn't be bothered to put her bra on. I can begin to laugh about such things now, which is a good sign that I'm beginning to accept that I only have one. Like a Cyclops with one eye, I am a Booblops!

Jayne and I headed home on the train, giggling about the day we'd just had and how we're itching to see the results. By the time I arrived home, I was absolutely shattered. It's an experience I'll never forget and, though it has drained me, it was so very worthwhile for my self-esteem, and to help me move forward on this journey.

CRASH! Thursday to Sunday was spent in a blur, if I'm honest. I managed to get myself together to go to a routine dentist appointment, but that was about all I could muster. I was more fatigued than I've ever felt in my life. Climbing the stairs was a real effort and a short walk on Sunday left me needing to rest again. My bones ached like they were going to break, and my appetite disappeared. I had a strange taste in my mouth and a return of mouth ulcers, not a pretty sight at all. I had experienced this initially when treatment began, but I thought I'd escape another bout.

I spent most of those 4 days sleeping, either in bed or curled up on the sofa, while the rest of the family carried on with their normal routines around me. I felt so guilty that I wasn't pulling my weight. Gus told me that was totally ridiculous and reminded me no one was expecting me to do anything. It's still hard when you're used to being on the go and have to stop, but I knew the best thing was to rest and that I'd recover better and more quickly if I did. So, I read, watched TV and slept. I hoped that, by Monday, I would be starting to feel better.

Some people might say I was mad to go off to the Sussex coast for a photo shoot 2 days after my treatment, but hey, you only get to live once. If an opportunity arises and you're able to, then just DO IT! I never want to look back with regrets or wish I'd taken the bull by the horns and done something. Now is the time to prove to myself that I can.

# Sixth Cycle – Week 2

## Monday, 3–Sunday, 9 October 2016

This week started off not so good, but it ended on a positive. As usual, there is always a positive to be found in the midst of a black cloud! A rainbow often follows a storm.

Monday, Tuesday and Wednesday were the days when I struggled most to do the simplest of tasks. I was so very tired even after a good night's sleep. That in itself plays with the mind. How could I be so tired after a night's sleep? I started to wonder whether something else was going on in my body. Of course, it wasn't, it was just the powerful drugs doing their job. But the tiredness coupled with the dreadful tummy upset again was enough to make anyone question their health.

My work colleague Karen dropped round on Monday. She always makes me feel better. We decided that 2016 has been a bad year for both of us and that, surely, 2017 will bring some positivity and sunshine. Neither of us will ever be the same again after what we've been through – we are changed forever. This is, of course, not all negative, because there will be positive changes for both of us too. We'll be stronger and more determined to live life to the full. And she brought homemade cookies, always a positive in my eyes, even though I could only nibble on one. I would make up for it in the coming days.

I managed to drag myself to the shops to stock up the fridge, but I had to cancel several lunch dates this week because I just wasn't up to it. I treated my wonderful mum to a hairdresser's appointment as my sister was away on holiday this week and wouldn't be around to do her hair. It was good to see my hairdresser, Claire, and we joked about what colour and texture my hair will be when it grows back. It's like baby fluff at the moment, but I'm guessing it won't be my old-style highlighted blonde and straight when it grows through. No, I'm going for mousey with a streak of silver-grey and curly, probably. I'll look like my mum in the eighties!

By Thursday, I was feeling more like my old self again, so I got to the breakfast meeting with my work colleagues. It was lovely to spend time with them, and I'm looking forward to a time when I can go back to work, feeling fully fit again. I've taken it upon myself to organise the Christmas night out for everyone, and that, in itself, makes me feel part of the group.

I worked from home this week; I answered emails and reviewed some of the work done with several of my young people. It's a good way of staying in the loop, at least. I have a few training sessions booked and a conference to attend in London with my co-worker in the next month, so that will help. I know it's unrealistic for me to return to my full-time job until my treatment ends, and I feel comfortable and happy, but I also want to stay in touch as much as I can.

I have struggled to communicate to work what is really going on and how I really feel. It's that fear of letting others down, the not wanting people to know that, hey, I can be vulnerable too. Silly, I know, but that's just me.

I know now that I need to let my guard down and tell it like it is. Yes, I can be brave, strong and resilient, but I'm also very human and can feel lost, sad, vulnerable, angry, scared and irrational about the future. I am determined to go back to work fit and healthy and with a mindset that lets me concentrate on the job. That way I will be an asset and not a liability.

After breakfast, I went off to Crazy Hats. It's always such a tonic for me and I'll miss going when I return to work. Maybe I can have an early lunch now and then and still attend. I was only there for a matter of minutes when Elaine, the therapist, whisked me away for a reflexology session, absolute bliss. She really is excellent at what she does. I'm looking forward to her relaxation class next week too. It helps in lots of ways and I've tried to use the techniques at home if I feel overwhelmed by anything. It's a good way to relax and de-stress. Nothing can be that bad, but the mind is so powerful it can escalate things to new levels and, believe me, my mind has.

On Friday, Gus and I went off to London for a night away. I booked this at the beginning of my chemotherapy sessions knowing this would be my treat at the end. We stayed in the Guorman Tower hotel in a room overlooking Tower Bridge – it was absolutely stunning. The room they gave us only had a river view, so the new confident version of me called reception and made a bit of a fuss. The result? We were moved to a room within touching distance of the bridge. I'm so proud of myself. And there was no extra charge when I went to pay the supplement the next day.

We had lunch at the First Dates restaurant, the Paternoster Chop House, near St Paul's, which was sublime. They even brought over a plate of fancy chocolates with Happy Birthday written in chocolate. I hadn't the heart to tell them it wasn't my birthday – no idea where they came up with that one. It was a fitting celebration.

London Oct 2016

In the evening, I got us tickets to see the Carole King show, Beautiful. I think Gus was a bit unsure about it, but at the end he said he enjoyed it much more than he thought he would. It was a fantastic musical, and it makes me realise how much I enjoy live music and performance – there is no substitute.

Saturday was spent walking for miles and miles, from Tower Bridge to Westminster and back again with everything in between: HMS Belfast, Borough Market, The Globe Theatre, The Clink Prison Museum, St Paul's, The Old Bailey and numerous coffee shops and restaurants. Got to keep my sustenance up. We arrived home after 11 p.m. and literally fell into bed; we were completely shattered.

No lie-in on Sunday either though, as I wanted to get over to Sibson airfield to watch my fellow breast cancer buddy Sarah Barnes do a skydive for Crazy Hats. It was a beautiful sunny day with a biting wind. She was on load three so we didn't have to wait too long for her jump. I still can't believe she had the balls to do it. It made me feel physically sick seeing her climb into the plane. It was utterly amazing to watch, and I managed to get a few decent shots as she made her descent strapped to a professional.

There were a few of us there to support her, so we decided we needed to celebrate with her afterwards. We all met up at a pub nearer home and had a couple of glasses of fizz. What an amazing woman. It has made me think that I need a challenge for the future. Skydiving wouldn't be my choice though. I don't think I could ever overcome my fear of falling! Georgia was with us and Sarah's son George – they've decided to do it next year for the charity. Oh my goodness, can I watch my own daughter do that?

Sarah raised over £1,000 for the charity, so she has done amazingly. I'm so proud of her for doing that.

My old school friend Lucy and her hubby, Neal, met us at the pub too. She had positive news about the nodules on the outside of her lung, which turned out to be chicken pox scars. Her operation has been re-scheduled for a couple of weeks so, hopefully, she and I will finish our awful journeys together, and we can look forward to a happy Christmas. It was so great to see her looking well and feeling well.

There is always hope, something that has probably got us both through the dark times. From the moment we are born, we are dying, but it's something we rarely give much thought to until something big happens. It's frightening and scary and no one truly wants to die. Yes, it's inevitable, eventually, but it won't be for a long time yet if we have anything to do with it!

Live, love, laugh and appreciate every single breath you take.

# Sixth Cycle – Week 3

Monday, 10–Sunday, 16 October 2016

The next part of the treatment journey begins today. I went to Northampton General Hospital for the planning appointment in readiness to begin radiotherapy treatment. I was taken into a room by one of the radiographers, and she explained the whole process to me – what to expect and any side effects I might have afterwards. The best thing was, I heard no mention of nausea.

Nausea has been the hardest thing to live with, and I empathise with anyone who suffers from morning sickness during pregnancy! It was the one thing that worried me most about having my own children – not the labour or the stretch marks, not even the sleep deprivation and the years of nurturing afterwards. No, it was the fear of nausea and sickness.

So, radiotherapy should be painless, and the only real side effects could be a sunburn feeling and tiredness in the weeks after treatment. That's music to my ears. I can cope with those side effects with E45 cream and rest.

I was then taken into the scanning room where I was positioned on the table under a huge polo mint-shaped machine. When I was positioned perfectly, the radiographers left the room, and the machine whirred and clanked around my body. It was all done in minutes.

Next came the tattooing. I now have three freckle-size tattoos across my chest area, which will be used to line me up perfectly every time I go for a treatment. Some people have been alarmed by this, but I'm not bothered by them. They are tiny dots anyway, and if it means the treatment is hitting the right area, I'm more than happy to have them. Those three dots, along with my scar, will be my constant reminder that I'm still here and breathing. That is the most important thing in the world to me, and I never want to forget that I have conquered this battle in life.

I must have 15 treatments over a 3 week period, which will mean travelling to Northampton daily from Monday to Friday. I've asked for early appointments to avoid the traffic, and to get a parking space. It will also mean I won't have to wait around too long as they won't be running late at that time of the day, fingers crossed. The treatment is due to start at the end of the month, so I'm hoping I'll be finished by the end of November.

As this is Week 3 of the cycle, I'm beginning to feel a bit more normal and my energy levels are good. That usually means that I try to pack every minute of the day with something, and this week has been no exception.

My manager came to see me on Tuesday, and I was able to talk frankly about how I'm feeling and what lies ahead for me. I'm still not certain when I'll feel ready to return to work at the office as I don't know how this part of the treatment will impact me. We decided not to make any firm decisions right now but agreed to meet up again next week when I've had my appointments. We could then make a plan for my return.

I have thought about this during the week, and I think I have an idea that will benefit the service and give me the chance to integrate myself back into my role. I don't want to drag my heels, but equally, I don't want to rush things and regret my actions later. I feel much more positive after today's meeting, though.

I have tried to spend more time with the girls this week, fitting around their schoolwork, jobs and social lives; that's no mean feat. Gus and I attended the sixth form intake evening with Phoebe on Tuesday. I was greeted with a hug from the school Head. So many people have been genuinely concerned for me and for my family, and it's been a huge support for us. I think we left there overwhelmed by the choice of subjects on offer. Hopefully, Phoebe has a much better idea than us. She has exams this week and has spent every spare hour revising.

I've spoken to her about not getting stressed and the importance of downtime. She kept saying that all she wanted was to make us proud. That made me cry, and I had to explain that we'll always be proud of her, and that she doesn't have to work so hard that she makes herself poorly. She seemed to take this on board but still has her head in a book constantly.

On Wednesday, I tested my stamina to the limit by letting Georgia take me shopping in Leicester for the day. We were on our feet all day except for coffee breaks and lunch, so by the time we got home, I was pretty much fit to drop. We had a busy day together doing normal things Mums and daughters do. It was great. I made sure I had dinner before vegging out on the sofa to recharge the batteries.

I have returned to badminton and yoga this week too. It was a good feeling to be well enough to take part and be a part of some different groups. I've also started dead lifting again in the garage gym at home. I've started with low weights, but it's a work in progress. I think, by Christmas, I should easily be able to lift the giant turkey out of the oven.

There was a relaxation class at Crazy Hats on Thursday, which I enjoyed very much. It's amazing what 30 minutes of letting your thoughts go can do. Visualisation is one of my favourite things and though I can discipline myself to do it alone, it's so much better doing it with a group. I would love to introduce this to some of the young people I work with because it would open their minds to things they can have control over. That's something to think about.

On Friday, I went into work to do some training for a couple of hours. It was good to be part of the team again, and I have absolutely no worries about slotting in when I go back. They are my work colleagues, but they're also my friends, and they make me feel like I've never been away. That's pretty amazing considering I'd only worked for the service for a year.

I'm so lucky. I hear people moan about their work and the folk they have to work alongside. I have none of that – I love my job, and I enjoy the company of the people I work with. I was shattered later in the day and hadn't realised what an impact going into work would have. Maybe it was the adrenaline beforehand? It was worth the tiredness.

The rest of the week was spent doing 'nice' things. A good friend took me out for lunch, and I had a visit from an old school friend later in the day. They're both so supportive and good company too.

Gus and I went to see the comedian Russell Kane on Friday evening. I haven't laughed so hard for ages. At one point, I was crying. He was hilarious, quick-witted and has so much energy. It was fantastic and just what I needed.

On Saturday, I woke up feeling like Wonder Woman. I decided to do some chopping and weeding in the garden. Three hours later, mission complete. I looked like the wild woman of Borneo, and I was supposed to be taking my husband out for lunch. A quick shower and change and we made it to the pub in time for a relaxing meal. We rarely do this at lunchtime, but it may be something we should do more regularly, bank balance permitting.

The rest of the weekend was spent relaxing, visiting family, watching a film and doing little else. The perfect end to the week.

Positives for this week:

My taste buds are almost back to their former selves, and I'm enjoying food again (better watch what the scales have to say about that).

I have returned to badminton and yoga – yay!

Radiotherapy treatment is about to begin.

My hair is growing back although it's very fine at the moment.

I can see a light at the end of what seemed like a very long tunnel.

No matter what life throws at you, there will always be a positive in there somewhere. It's true that sometimes you'll have to dig deep to find that positive, but it will be there. Personally, when things are on the up and life is looking settled for a while, I'm going to appreciate every positive and not just skip on past it without giving it a thought. I'm banking all those positives to help me through any rough seas ahead.

No more cycles.

## Monday, 17–Sunday, 23 October 2016

Well, I've finally made it. This week sees the end of the cycles. If I'd been having another poisoning, it would have been today, Monday, 17 October 2016, but the 6 Cycles are all complete. The cancer-zapping army has completed its work and is no longer needed to march around my body in a Laser Quest style, destroying all the nasty cells that may have slipped through the net and gone fugitive. I can almost hear my healthy cells screaming, 'Hoorah!' At last they don't need to run and hide and can replicate to their hearts' content. Hopefully, this will ensure I return to my normal healthy resting state and can continue to live my life and enjoy it to the full. It's been a tough 4 months and is not something I'd want to have to do again. I wouldn't wish it on anyone either, but it has been manageable with the support of everyone around me.

There has been so much support and kindness, and I truly know now how very lucky I am. What an amazing lot you all are. To quote Morgan Freeman in Evan Almighty, 'It takes just one act of random kindness (ark).' I've received many acts of random kindness this year from such a wealth and breadth of people. These gestures haven't always been big, but they have been huge to me.

To quote but a few:

When my good friend and walking buddy, Diane, drove a 24-mile round trip, twice, just to make sure I had false eyelashes for the photo shoot last month. I didn't have a clue what to look for in the shops, so she gave me a collection of her unused lashes. What a star.

The unexpected note through the post from a friend far away that just says, 'You can do this girl.' It reduced me to tears.

The stranger who pulled up in her car and got out to introduce herself as she'd heard from another friend that I had been poorly. She wanted to lend her support, how lovely.

Yesterday, the neighbour that came across to ask how Gus was doing, as much as how I was doing. I'm conscious of how the last 6 months have affected Gus and the girls and the rest of my close family, but it's really heartening to know others think of them too.

There are many, many more incidents that I could name, and not a day goes by that something doesn't make me sit up and take note. Humanity is basically warm and good-natured, something we sometimes lose sight of in our busy lives.

No chemotherapy today, but I had an appointment with the oncologist. I was hoping it would be Dr Rabina, and my wishes were granted. I do like my oncologist, Dr Milanovich, but I feel I have a better rapport with Dr Rabina. I'm comfortable asking questions, and I never feel rushed by him. He was more than happy with my progress and set my mind at rest about a few things. We talked about my finger and toenails, the return to normality of the digestive system and the bruising around my scar tissue.

All of my worries are linked to the concoctions that have been pumped into my system, and the bruising turned out to be shadows as I look down at my chest area. I talked about my fears of the cancer returning or appearing somewhere else, and he allayed these fears. He said my acceptance and positive attitude have helped my recovery, and that cancer will always be at the back of my mind, but that is where it should stay.

He said he could be knocked over by a bus on his way home tonight, but he can't let that thought cloud his present. I get what he was trying to say, and I will endeavour to adopt this approach in the coming months and years. I am 99.5% positive most of the time, but I do have those dark thoughts now and again – I'm only human. Once you've been touched by something as big as this, I don't think you can ever convince yourself you'll continue to stay cancer-free. Dr Rabina was adamant that my positivity was the single best thing to help with my wellbeing, with my physical and psychological recovery, and I have to agree with him.

It reminded me of a lady I taught floristry to years ago, who was married to a doctor. If she, or one of their three children, got up in the morning and said they felt unwell, her husband would say, 'Try saying that again in a more upbeat voice and I'm sure you'll feel better.' I used to think that was cruel, but actually, he had a point. If I were to use my whiney voice and speak in low tones about how I've felt in the past few months, I could make myself feel miserable, but when I use my upbeat voice, I do feel more positive and all-conquering.

I left the Centenary Wing and Dr Rabina feeling full of life and ready to tackle the next phase of my treatment, which is due to start towards the end of next week.

After my appointment, my sister, Alison, did a reiki treatment for me. It was so relaxing and I drifted off to sleep during the process. I can remember feeling warmth around my head, shoulders, knees and feet and seeing bright turquoise and, later, white light. Apparently, it took three attempts to wake me up! I was definitely enjoying the rest. She had spent time around my head and said how, initially, it had felt chaotic. No doubt, those were my thoughts surrounding the hospital appointment and the coming week! I've never had a reiki treatment before, but I can't wait for the next one now.

I tried to spend Tuesday resting as much as possible, and I went to my niece Hannah's shop, The Beauty Bug in Raunds, to have my finger and toenails painted. Dr Rabina had advised this would be a good thing to do as some of my nails have turned black, blue, yellow and every shade in between. I know I'm eventually going to lose some of the nails because of the potency of the drugs I've taken, but being able to cover them with nail polish for the time being makes a big difference to my self-confidence. They're now a pretty shade of pale pink, courtesy of Hannah. I did reverse the restful phase later by returning to badminton. Two hours of running around a badminton court certainly tested my stamina, but I think I did okay and I slept like a baby.

Wednesday and Thursday were also going to test me as I needed to get back into work mode. I was up and out of the house at 6:30 a.m. on Wednesday to catch the train to London with Alex, my other half in the Substance Misuse field, for a work-related conference. On the whole, it was a good day, even though much of the material wasn't specific enough for our roles. By lunchtime, I was getting tired and struggled to keep my enthusiasm. It was good to spend the day with Alex. It reminded me of the excellent rapport we have, and the ability to see the funny side of things, especially being stalked by a couple of other delegates. I arrived home at 6:30 p.m. and just about managed to eat dinner before I needed my bed again.

On Thursday, I was out of the house and on my way to the office for supervision with my manager and training on a newly issued laptop. Cath and I only had a short time together, but we managed to discuss the necessary points and agree a time frame and strategy for going forward. I feel much happier and confident that I'll be able to make a gradual but purposeful return to my position, and that it won't be that far away either. I had over an hour's training with a very patient man before being handed a brand spanking new laptop to help me in my role. It's a laptop that becomes a tablet, and I'm excited as I'll be able to use it to take notes and draw pictures. It will be a fantastic tool to use with those young people who aren't always good at putting their thoughts into words. Being able to draw and use mind maps will be an asset to my role, I'm sure. I was very tired after the training, but I think that was down to information overload.

I met my friend Lucy afterwards for lunch and came back to life. It was great to see her, and we joked about how well we both look, and that no one would believe us if we told them what we'd been through and what we still have to come. She's going into hospital next week for her second operation and then hopefully, after a period of recovery, she'll be able to return to normality. My gut feeling is that everything will be good this time around, and we can look forward to many happy times at the beach together.

I was pretty tired on Friday, but I managed to spend a bit of time shopping with Georgia before going out for an Indian meal with the Crazy Hat girls, or as Gus likes to call us, 'the

Mad Hatters.' We spent the night laughing so much that my sides hurt. I left the restaurant and glanced at my mobile only to realise I had messages and missed calls from home.

The first one was to say Phoebe was on her way to the hospital with her dad! The last was to say they were already home. I rushed home to find Gus in agony with toothache. He could hardly hold a conversation. He'd been told by Kettering hospital staff that he needed to go to Northampton General for an emergency dental appointment. They had given him codeine for the pain and sent him away. I called Northampton before racing over there. It was a good job I did as there's no emergency dental service there either. I was told to call 111 for advice on emergency treatment.

After what seemed like hours on the phone, I was given two numbers to call at 8 a.m. the next day, which meant we had 8 hours to wait. Poor Gus spent the night sipping iced water every 30 seconds to numb the pain. He did get to an emergency dentist the next day and was given antibiotics as there was an infection under the filling our dentist had put in a couple of days before. Poor old Gus spent the weekend in pain, and we had to cancel a dinner date with our friends. I knew he must feel pretty awful as he never so much as takes a paracetamol when he has a headache. Over the weekend, he was popping ibuprofen, paracetamol, codeine and antibiotics. I'm happy to say that, by Sunday evening, he was looking a lot brighter and actually eating again.

The shoe was on the other foot this weekend, and after 6 months of taking care of me, I was able to take care of him. It has certainly made me realise what a fantastic partner I have in him. He has never once complained about looking after me, and I must have been a right pain at times.

So, what a blessing it is to have a husband like Gus and two fantastic daughters like Georgia and Phoebe. What a blessing it is to have a fantastic close family and a myriad of supporting and loving friends. I may never win the National Lottery but I have won in the lottery of life so far.

# The Next Stage

## Monday, 24 October–Friday, 4 November 2016

I've left it longer than a week to complete the next entry of the blog because things feel so much more relaxed now. Chemotherapy has ended, and the side effects it left behind have finally begun to fade. I'm so glad I've written this blog as it will always serve to remind me of what I have experienced. Like anything, time softens pain and upset; those who have experienced childbirth know this only too well. I remember a hospital porter wheeling me to the ward after I'd given birth to Georgia, and he asked me when I planned to have my second child. I said, 'NEVER!'

It's amazing how time helped me view her birth as near-perfect and forget any of the not so good parts. It's the same with cancer treatment except I've kept a written record to remind me of how it actually was. This is not for me to dwell on and revisit but rather to give some accuracy to the events, so I never forget how lucky I am to have had the treatment that gave me the chance to carry on living.

It was half term this week, and I wanted to spend as much time as possible with the girls. It's not often I can take a week off to do this, so it was an ideal opportunity, and I tried to keep my time free for the girls. Phoebe and I spent a couple of afternoons at the orthodontist, and her braces have been removed. She has beautifully straight teeth and a gorgeous smile!

The girls and I celebrated with afternoon tea and, as this was paid for as a treat by my friend, Angela, I pushed the boat out, and we had a bottle of Prosecco too. Very naughty on a Tuesday afternoon, but why not? I've spent my life doing things in a right and proper manner. Where is the harm in breaking some of the rules? We had a super afternoon, and it was great to spend time with them on my own. They're such fantastic company, they talk non-stop (guess those of you who know me will say they inherited that from me), and they make me laugh.

I'm so glad we made the decision to have children. It was never really on my agenda for life and once I got to the age of 30, I honestly thought it would never be a reality. It took Gus being deployed to Kenya for a few months while he was serving in the army, for us to realise something was missing from our lives. Georgia Madaleine arrived a year after Gus returned from Africa, and Phoebe Harriet arrived 3 years later. Our little family was complete. Time has flown and I now understand what people mean when they say you should make the most of every day with your children. It seems like yesterday that they were toddling around the garden, and now they're both young ladies, beginning to make their own way in the world. I'm so proud of what they've become, and I feel so lucky to have been blessed with two healthy, happy, joyful children.

My friend Lucy had her operation this week, and I have anxiously waited for news about her. She has undergone a 'sleeve lobectomy' where the surgeon has removed half of one of her lungs. I went to see her in hospital a few days after the operation and was surprised at how well she looked. A few days later, she had the histology report, and the cancer has gone. The relief I felt was palpable, so goodness only knows how it felt for her and her family. I'm hoping this has just been a bad year for us, and we can look forward to a brighter future, and a lengthy one.

I started radiotherapy treatment this week, which is a bit surreal. It's painless and so far, there haven't been any real side effects. I have felt tired, but that could be more to do with the fact that I try to squash 48 hours into 24, every day. The treatment is all so high-tech; lying on the bed with the radiographers talking co-ordinates over my head, moving the trolley right, left, up and down until they're confident the three dots are in perfect alignment. Having to lie perfectly still sounds easy until you have to do it. How many times have I thought I'm going to sneeze, or I have an itch behind my ear.

It's over in minutes and all that remains is to get dressed and drive home. Each time, the radiographer has drawn on me with black marker pen, and every day I'm in the bath trying to scrub it off gently. I don't want them to think I don't wash every day. It's such a non-invasive, silent treatment that I even asked the radiographer if it was a placebo treatment. That made him laugh, at least. He said they don't usually tell people, but as I'd guessed it, he could tell me the truth. I know, as the treatment progresses, I may experience some side effects, but at the moment, apart from the tiredness and my skin being a bit tender, that's it. Thank goodness, it's nothing like chemotherapy.

Gus had a day off this week, so we spent the day together as a family. This involved eating lots and walking for a few miles with the hounds. They may be simple things, like conversation and enjoying one another's company, but they are the things that make life rich.

The weekend was busy, with a charity quiz night where we managed to come fourth out of six teams, so we didn't disgrace ourselves completely, and a night out to see The Fallen Mavericks (Georgia's friends' band), an excellent night of music and dancing – what talented lads. I'm looking forward to seeing their names in lights one day. A Sunday roast at my gorgeous florist, and fellow Capricorn friend, Lisa's home. She makes the best roast dinner ever, and I always eat too much because it's so very yummy. There is nothing better than sitting round the table with family and good friends, sharing a meal, making a perfect end to the week.

Halloween and the first full week of radiotherapy.

Halloween face!

Halloween was another reminder of how our girls have grown. They no longer get excited about trick or treating, the dressing up and bags full of sweets and chocolates. Gus carved a pumpkin, and as soon as it got dark I put it out at the front of the house on a little stool. It was like moths to a flame. Within minutes we had our first customers. There was a steady stream of children at the door, all dressed beautifully in costumes, and by 7:30 p.m. I had to blow out the candle and bring the pumpkin indoors as I'd run out of sweets. It was a great evening and so uplifting to see how much effort the children and their parents had gone to.

Most of my treatment appointments have been early morning and on time this week, so I've been able to fit other things in for the rest of the day. I've had lunch out, had a neighbour round for tea and cake and managed to finish the acupuncture paperwork for work.

My neighbour is 85 years young, and she does make me laugh. She's been a widow for over 40 years, but she has lived her life to the full. She still takes two or three holidays abroad every year with a friend, and she's always got a smile on her face. She is so positive and if she comes up against an obstacle, she finds a way around it. I hope I can be like that at her age. We got talking about my treatment and the healthcare system and how things were when she was a child.

She brought me to tears as she recounted her time in hospital followed by a convalescence home when she had to have an operation on her ear as a young girl. There was no room for parents in those days, and she could only see them at visiting times. When she went to the convalescence home, she was only allowed a weekly visit from her parents. She told me how all the kids used to cry for their mothers at night, and how they weren't well cared for in the home.

When her parents visited her, they had a battle on their hands to take her home that day. She says her mother was horrified at the state of her cleanliness and the state of her clothes. She was unkempt and dirty. How things have changed – for the better, thank goodness. I hear people complain about our NHS, but I think we have little to moan about. I certainly have no issues. My treatment has been fantastic.

My friend Lisa, and goddaughter, Lillibet, took Phoebe and I to the theatre in Northampton to see Dirty Dancing. I must be the only person in the whole world who hasn't seen the film. Everyone I speak to is horrified at this as if I've missed out on an important component of life. Well, I'm okay now. I've seen the stage production, and I thoroughly enjoyed it. It's a shame we've lost Patrick Swayze. I'm going to ask Father Christmas for a copy of the film on DVD. I hope this will absolve me from the hall of shame.

We invited my work colleague Karen and her husband round on Friday evening for a meal. It's been months since I've felt up to cooking, let alone cooking for other people. It was a cathartic thing for me to do and has given me some confidence in my ability to prepare something edible!

They've had a particularly difficult time this year, losing their youngest son in a tragic accident. I cannot begin to imagine how that felt, and how they are coping. I do know that our situations this year have brought Karen and I together in the strangest of ways, and I know I've made a friend for life. We had a really good evening, one I will look forward to repeating. It's odd how life twists and turns, giving us endless opportunities, even in difficult times.

And that's how I will end this entry, on a positive. Of all the bad things life throws in our way, we can pretty much guarantee there will be a positive in there, somewhere. It's just a question of looking.

# The Journey Continues

## November 2016

How great is it that I now feel I can stretch my blog writing for longer periods? This time it has been almost a month. Lots has happened, but it doesn't feel nearly as intense. Things must be improving.

I completed my 15 radiotherapy appointments this month. The treatment was completely different to the chemotherapy, and I hardly knew anything was being done. It was a little surreal. All I did was turn up every day, lie on a bed while the radiographers lined up the beam, positioning me precisely on the table; a few millimetres this way, a few millimetres that way, up a bit, down a bit. Just like an episode of the Golden Shot. Now I'm really showing my age!

I was told to expect side effects, which would take a while to appear. I first noticed the itching and redness 5 or 6 days later. This has got progressively worse and is probably at its height now, around 2 weeks after the last treatment. It's bearable but uncomfortable, like sunburn, or for those of us who've ever been heavy-handed with a razor when shaving our legs, razor burn!

The most tender part is under my arm, which I guess doesn't see the sun too often and is therefore more sensitive. At the moment, I only wear a bra if I really have to as it's too painful; crop tops are my new best friends! Before all of this kicked off, I wouldn't have dreamed of leaving the house without the correct 'support', but these days, I've thrown caution to the wind. I only have one breast that needs support anyway, and I think she's quite happy in a pretty, semi-supportive Lycra T-shirt. I bet it's a blessed relief not to have a bloody wire cupping you all day!

During my 15 days toing and froing from the hospital, I met up with the same people waiting for their blasting. I will never forget sitting in the waiting room and hearing the breaking news that Trump had won the election in America. The news was met with an element of disbelief by us all, but in the grand scheme of things, we agreed we had more important issues to think about. It's amazing how you build rapport and camaraderie with other human beings, despite our plights. I guess this was never truer than when the soldiers played football in no man's land on Christmas Day in World War 1. There is nothing more life-affirming than the coming together of kindred spirits.

There was one particular gentleman who will remain in my memory for a long time. His name is Raymond, and he is 86 years old. He's a spritely, smartly dressed gentleman with a wonderful, positive attitude. Raymond has throat cancer but was told by his GP it was easily treated. He underwent 20 radiotherapy treatments and an endless stream of other appointments on a daily basis.

On one occasion, the radiographer called his name, and she carried what I can only describe as a mesh mask, approximately 60 cm square, with the imprint of a head on it. I asked Raymond about this the next day, and he told me the imprint was of his own head. The mesh is placed over him then bolted to the bed to make sure his head is kept perfectly still during treatment.

It all sounded very Silence of the Lambs to me, but he said it was no big deal. Apparently, he asked if he could keep the mesh thing afterwards. He thought it would be useful for straining Brussel sprouts at Christmas! What a sense of humour!

I didn't spend too long with Raymond, but in the short time we chatted, I got to know so much about his life. On the day of my last treatment, a 7:30 a.m. appointment, I arrived to find the doors still locked. Raymond was sitting in his car and beckoned me over. I sat in the warm car with him while he told me how he'd been getting up at 4 a.m. every day to get ready. He started his 20-mile journey at 6 a.m. to make sure he could get a parking space at the hospital. His appointment that day wasn't until 8:20 a.m. – bless him.

That last day was very emotional, and Raymond's life story added to this. He told me how he'd lost his wife 7 years earlier, and how his stepson had helped them move to a more suitable property nearby in Desborough, and how, after they moved to be closer to family, his stepson had moved to southern Ireland! Raymond described his wife, Jean, as the love of his life but said he hadn't married her until he was 46 years old.

Apparently, he was sweet on her as a young man, but he went off to do his national service and then war broke out. He never wrote to Jean during that time, which he regrets, and when he returned home, she had married someone else. At this point, I was almost in tears. One day, he found himself wandering in Edmonton and passed her parent's home. He knocked on the front door and was invited in by Jean's mother. She told him that, although Jean was married, the marriage wasn't a good one. Raymond left a telephone number for Jean, and she called that night. The rest was history.

I asked what he'd done in-between returning from the war and being reunited with Jean. He said he'd never married or had a serious relationship because Jean was his only love. They had 32 wonderful years together, and he says he misses her every single day. What a true love story theirs was. From his perspective, at 86, he's on borrowed time. As I left that day, I passed him a slip of paper with our address and phone number and said if he was ever passing, he was more than welcome to pop in for a cup of tea and a chat. He seemed genuinely pleased by this suggestion, so I hope he turns up at my door soon.

The last few weeks have flown by. I have been, and still am, sore and tired, but it is to be expected. This has been a journey like no other I've had to face. It has made me re-evaluate everything in my life and to really look at myself inside and out. I have done more reflection in the past 7 months than I ever did in 4 years of training as a counsellor.

I've learnt things about myself. I always thought that, God forbid, if I was ever diagnosed with cancer I'd crumble into a mess or disappear and sit out my days gazing at the ocean.

I've learnt that I can tackle things head on, and I have got a certain amount of resilience and strength when I need it. My family and friends are the backbone of all of this fight, and they have been there for me every step of the way.

I don't think, actually, I know, it wouldn't have been the same journey without them.

Georgia, Fizz & Dave
sleeping Oct 2016

Strangely, I passed hearses on the A14 three times during this part of the treatment programme. I couldn't believe how emotional I got each time. One of the hearses in particular stands out in my memory – the coffin inside was plain, with no flowers. There were no black limousines following, and it upset me to think of someone passing away and no one being there to mourn them.

The positive I took each time I saw a hearse was how respectful we are of a life's passing; the traffic slowed as it passed a cortège. Each time this made me cry because it made me realise we all have that respect for another person, no matter whether their funeral is frugal or lavish. A funeral cortège is a reminder of the fragility of life. There is no escape for any of us.

There were plenty of positive, happy stories from the last few weeks, too. My dear friend Lucy has got the all clear from her consultant and is now cancer-free. I sobbed at this news. We've been such a part of each other's stories for the past few months, and there have been dark times, times when I've wondered whether she'd have a happy ending. There have been times when I've felt guilty that my journey hasn't been as fraught with difficulties. I know what she'll say when she reads this, but it is so difficult to watch one of your friends go through so much. There is a happy story now although we both agree there are no guarantees (and that's the same for every human on the planet). We will appreciate every day just that little bit more than before.

I was asked to take part in a trial at the hospital and, after reading all of the literature, decided to go ahead. I had to have a blood test and take part in a cognitive function test. I am now in the control period and if I suffer no side effects, I'll be put into one of 3 groups – those taking 100 mg of aspirin daily, 300 mg of aspirin daily and a placebo group. There is evidence to suggest that daily aspirin can prevent cancers returning. If this aids someone in the future, then it's a small thing to have done. I will be monitored for 5 years on this programme.

I've already been prescribed my first month's supply of Tamoxifen, which I've been taking for 10 days. I'll be on this drug for 10 years as my tumour was oestrogen receptive. It's early days, but I haven't experienced any real side effects yet, and perhaps I won't, ever.

I've had various social events this month, and it has been great to feel well enough to attend. Gus and I had a night away in Lincoln to celebrate the end of this treatment phase. It was uplifting to wander around without an agenda and simply enjoy each other's company. It ended up being a cheap date as I had had too many glasses of red wine, fell asleep, and missed our dinner date. I'd forgotten that my wine tolerance level was probably at an all-time low, so those three or four glasses of particularly quaffable Shiraz soon took effect. Luckily, we'd bought crisps and biscuits with us, so Gus enjoyed them watching Sunday evening TV. He woke me up at 11:15 p.m. I had no hangover and went back to sleep, but by golly did I scoff my full English the next morning.

December is always a busy month, and this year will be no different with lots of things planned: a party for the Famous Five plus one (my old school mates – Lucy, Louise, Sally, Jane and Kurt) at my house to celebrate life; the first choir practice at Crazy Hats (watch this space); my work Christmas party, tobogganing at Stamford; a week in Devon with our good friends, the Colleys and lots more impromptu events in between. Normality is slowly returning to the Paton household – yippee.

I'm also planning to return to the office this month. Big step for me, I know. I have been doing bits and bobs from home, but it's not the same as being in your place of work. I plan to take it slowly on the run up to Christmas to make sure I don't set myself back in any way. Lots of friends and colleagues have said I should wait until the new year, but I think the next few weeks will give me a sense of normality and let me dip my toe in the water of work again. That way, January won't feel so scary. I know it's a long road, and I've been off work with more than a cold, but everyone has to start somewhere and this will be my somewhere.

Christmas is on the horizon, I can almost smell it. The decorations have been brought down from the loft, and it's on my agenda to have the house looking like Santa's grotto by the weekend. I love, love, love Christmas, and Christmas 2016 is going to be a very special one for this family.

Nicola Jane press release Dec 2016

This is a 'proof' from the Nicola Jane photo shoot ready for the January brochure. I wasn't sure if I was brave enough to include it, but then I remembered, I've just beaten the Big C.

# Christmas Has Arrived

## December 2016

Wow! I can't quite believe another month has passed by – time stops for no man or woman! It's been a busy month. I wanted to add another post before 2016 finally draws to a close in a few days' time, because I'll be glad to see the back of it

It's been a strange year, full of emotions, highs and lows, both personally and in the wider world.

To quote the Daily Express today: 'It is safe to say 2016 is a year which will go down in the history books as one of the most eventful in modern history.'

It seems as if there have been so many celebrity deaths this year – far more than in other years, and many have been people who've been part of my life. People like David Bowie and Alan Rickman, Terry Wogan, Ronnie Corbett, Prince, Ed Stewpot Stewart, Pete Burns, Caroline Aherne, Victoria Wood, Paul Daniels, Andrew Sachs, David Gest, Tony Warren, Robert Vaughan, Muhammed Ali, Gene Wilder, Rick Parfitt, Leonard Cohen and the latest, George Michael (which I still can't get my head around). So much talent, lost.

It's made me think about how very ordinary I actually am. I'm living on a planet with billions of people who are as ordinary and extraordinary as me. Life is fragile for all of us, and fame and money make no difference in the end. We leave this place the same way we entered it – with nothing but ourselves. All of these losses, some untimely, make me grateful to be here. I'm not untalented, but some of the people that have passed have been super talented and death has still taken them.

There have been times this year when I've had to face the possibility of death, but it hasn't happened, and I've been spared. I'm not deeply religious, but I do wonder about what we're all here for and what happens when we leave. I often think there's a huge control room somewhere, and we are little dots being pushed here and there to suit some other force. Who knows? Perhaps we never will, though I have a sneaking suspicion that, in time, we will have some answers.

Of course, this hasn't just been a year marred by celebrity deaths. It has also been a year of many terrorist attacks, which have claimed the lives of too many people. There have been devastating earthquakes, airline disasters and the awful Zika virus, all of which have claimed the lives of many people just like me, ordinary people, going about their business.

Cancer will have claimed the lives of many ordinary and extraordinary people this year. I am so very thankful it hasn't taken me, or my close friends, who've each had their own fights. I'm sure we'll all live and love a little harder now that we've had this experience. I know I will, and I know I don't get half as stressed about the little things as I used to. What's the point? Life is a precious gift that needs to be valued on a daily basis. I've always felt this to be true, but now, I believe it more than ever.

This year has been a sad year all round, and it feels as if everyone I've come into contact with has been touched with this emotion, but there have also been lots of positive things going on. December has been no exception.

The Crazy Hats charity has formed a choir, and I took part in the first rehearsal along with about thirty others. I'm not sure the choirmaster will get me up to scratch for a performance next year, but I'm willing to let her try. Singing is something I've always wanted to have a go at but never dared to try, but I have more courage these days. Singing is proven to be good for well-being, so where's the harm? Okay, okay, I know; everyone else's ears may suffer.

I returned to the office at the beginning of December. This is a huge positive for me and has been great for my self-esteem and my soul. I work with such a great bunch of people who have made me realise how I have been missed. I'm amazed at how quickly I've slotted back in, but it'll be a while before I'm back to full speed. It won't be long though.

I have been quite tired and have limited the number of hours I work, which was sensible. Concentration is the hardest. I can start a task and then, within a few minutes, I've lost the thread of what I'm doing. I'm sure this will improve over time, and I'll be back to my old self.

I think starting back just before the Christmas break was a good move as everyone is in high spirits and there have been several gatherings of everyone in one place, which doesn't normally happen. It has been good to socialise both at work and at organised functions. It has made me feel part of the team again after such a long time away from them all.

While I was away from the office, I helped organise the staff Christmas party, which was a gamble, but it turned out to be a success. It was great to go out and socialise with my colleagues as well as being back in an office setting with them. I've missed my job and my colleagues, and I'm looking forward to working alongside them all in 2017.

Cheeky Girls Christmas night out 2016

We had a street party this month to celebrate Christmas. After a similar event in the summer for the Queen's 90th birthday, we decided to try one at Christmas. It was a wonderful afternoon – the weather held, and we stayed out until way after dark. Everyone came. I think there were around forty of us, and we put up a small marquee, had fairy lights, hot food and mulled wine, with festive music. It was great to see everyone come together and celebrate.

I was exhausted by the end of it, but it was truly a wonderful afternoon. I hope the Christmas street party will become a tradition in Holmfield Drive.

Christmas Day was a family affair, and we spent it quietly with my parents. It was a special day with lots of present opening, good food and relaxing, just how it should be. I can't think of a Christmas Day I've enjoyed more.

Christmas Eve 2016

Gus & I Nov 2016

My hair is now growing back quite quickly – at least I have a full covering now, and it's beginning to look like a bad haircut rather than the result of chemotherapy! Many people have commented on the fact that it looks like it's going to be grey. Like that's something to be worried about, really? I couldn't care less if it was all the colours of the rainbow. I'd rather be alive with grey hair than dead with a full head of blonde highlights.

That being said, I know that as soon as it's okay to do so, I will return to my blonde highlighted self, because I want to look like me again. I feel as if the treatment has aged me 10 years when I see my reflection in the mirror, but I hold out hope that this may reverse itself now that I've finished with the drugs and have begun to come to terms with what has happened.

December has been a month free from any hospital appointments, which is a huge positive. Since April, I haven't had an appointment-free week, let alone month. My next appointment is at the Breast Care Unit to monitor the aspirin trial, and after that I'll see the oncologist at the end of January.

I guess he wants to see how I've got on with the Tamoxifen. So far, so good. I've been taking the drug for over 6 weeks now, and the only real issue I've had is with achy joints, especially the shoulders, upper arms and ankles. I'm not sure if this is directly related to the drug, so I hope the oncologist will have the answer to this. Other than that, I'm doing good.

So, although there have been some negatives this year, or as I prefer to think, a series of unfortunate events, there have also been many positives.

These include:

My circle of new friends has widened considerably.

I have rekindled lots of old friendships.

I am closer to my family.

My newfound confidence has spurred me to sing, model and even take to a canoe.

This blog, and now my book, has been my saviour at times, and I will sorely miss writing it. You see, even when life deals you bum cards, positivity will always shine through.

Fizz & Dave Oct 2016

# End of the 12-month Rollercoaster

## February 2017

## The new year

Life has returned to normal in the last few months. Gone are the days when I could sit and pour my innermost feelings into this blog. If I'm honest, I feel resentful of this time being withdrawn. I'd like to carry on with what I started, but I know this isn't practical and possibly not even therapeutic any more. It's time to move on and live my life as a well person again.

I had a follow-up appointment with the oncologist in the last few weeks. He told me, 'go and live your life.' He reassured me that once the mastectomy was done, I was cancer-free, and after the adjuvant treatment, I was free to do as I pleased; go on holiday, dye my hair and enjoy every moment. I was able to talk to him about the aches in some of my joints since starting the Tamoxifen, and he reassured me this is normal.

I've also had a niggling dull backache for a couple of months, and my GP has sent me for an x-ray to put my mind at rest. She was fairly certain it was a muscular issue as the pain comes and goes depending on the exercise I've done. The oncologist felt the same and has said I can go back at any time if I have any concerns, which is comforting to know. I don't want to jump to conclusions every time I have the slightest ache or pain, but it's difficult not to sometimes. Cancer is not at the forefront of my mind, but it is a floating cloud that regularly drifts across my thoughts. I hope this will become less and less prominent as time passes, and I won't be giving it as much space in my head.

I've resumed all of my normal exercise routines: badminton, yoga, dead lifting and dog walking. I have even started to introduce a 10-minute yoga routine when I get out of bed in the morning. It's made quite a difference to how the rest of my day goes as I feel brighter and energised at the start of the day.

I have started to concentrate on my diet now that I feel better. I've given myself a few months since the end of treatment to enjoy eating again, but now is the time to start to rein it in. I plucked up the courage to stand on the scales this week, and I wasn't particularly surprised to see I'd gained 10 lbs since my treatment ended. I've set myself a goal to lose that extra weight by continuing to eat sensibly and healthily.

I just need to cut out the crap. So, for the next few weeks, there will be no cakes, biscuits, sweets, crisps, chocolate or an abundance of bread and butter. My treat for the day will be a turmeric, ginger, cinnamon and black pepper latte, sweetened with honey. It probably sounds disgusting, but if you get the combination of ingredients just right, it's delicious.

I returned to work full-time in the last week of January. That was quite difficult as I was incredibly tired at the end of the day. I feel unsettled and a bit disillusioned with my area of work. I've always felt that the field of drug and alcohol work has a shelf life. Perhaps having a spell of time away has given me time to ponder the possibility of doing something else.

I've thought about doing some private flower work – weddings and parties. I have a pipe dream of owning a shop again, but I know that, in reality, it's a 24/7 career and I'm not sure I have the energy and commitment to take it on again. I was barely 19 last time, with no ties, so it was my life! I've thought of a couple of products that would help someone after a mastectomy, and I'm investigating how I can make them a reality. So, watch this space, maybe one day I'll be on Dragon's Den!

I've managed to get out and about a bit, taking full advantage of feeling well again. We had a week in Devon with friends, Gus and I had a night away at Wadenhoe House and, more recently, a trip to the Highlands to visit an old army colleague of his.

'Chemo brain' isn't a term I believed had any bearing on me until I tried to get us on a flight with my passport and one of my daughter's, rather than Gus's! Now, I am the sort of traveller who checks everything in triplicate, but for some reason this time, I didn't! The flight staff informed me that we didn't actually need passports to fly to Inverness in Scotland, but we did need a form of I.D. Apparently a driver's licence or a bank card would have sufficed.

I've also managed to lose my degree certificate, and it's made me wonder whether there could be something to this 'chemo brain' thing after all. I've had every cupboard, drawer and hiding place turned over at least three times, but to no avail – my degree certificate is gone. It's not the end of the world, I can have a reprint at a cost of £46.

The Highlands were beautiful. I was blown away by the vastness and the natural beauty of the place. We must have travelled 500 miles over the weekend, as our friends packed as much into our visit as possible: Loch Ness, Aviemore, Eilean Donan Castle, Ullapool and Skye. I would love to return in spring or summer to see the differences in the colours and scenery.

Scotland Feb 2017

The girls and I had a superb weekend in Birmingham to see Strictly Come Dancing – all sequins and glitter. Gus and I were treated to a spa day by the girls for Christmas. We had a wonderful day of pure relaxation, and I had a special massage for those who've been through cancer treatment.

Strictly Come Dancing Jan 2017

I have been away to the east coast with some of my girlfriends. It was the first time Lucy and I had been away together since we'd both completed treatment. It's hard to believe that this time last year, we were walking the same beach blissfully unaware of what would be coming for us in the year ahead. All I'm pleased about is that we've both got through it, and the future is there for the taking. Blessed I'd say.

For me, life is about looking forward now and planning things to make myself and my family happy.

So, here is my agenda for the next couple of months:

18 February 2017: my first hairdresser's appointment since my treatment ended.

24 February 2017: Pet Shop Boys concert with my mate Lisa.

26 February 2017: afternoon tea with my Crazy Hats mates.

28 February 2017: Gran Canaria with the family for a week.

Gran Canaria 2017

10 March 2017: ABBAmania with my Crazy Hats mates.

13 March 2017: Krakow with Georgia for a few days. Her present for doing so well with her A levels despite what was going on with me.

19 March 2017: a party to celebrate my parent's diamond wedding anniversary.

Mum & I March 2017

Mum & Dad 16 March 1957

60th wedding anniversary

1 April 2017: School of Rock theatre trip to mark the year anniversary of my diagnosis – I think a bottle of bubbly will be in order that day.

2 April 2017: Crazy Hats Charity Walk – my first one!

Crazy Hats Charity Walk April 2017

15 April 2017: Kefalonia for a week with my rock, Gus.

Kefalonia April 2017

Life is good.

This is bringing my blog to a natural close. I could go on and write, but I feel this part of the journey is now done, and the next part hopefully won't be as eventful. I started writing to help come to terms with the situation, and I'm certain it has been a positive and cathartic thing for me to have done. I hope that, in some small way, someone reading it will feel less frightened if they find themselves in the same situation. I wouldn't wish what I've gone through on my worst enemy, but it has been manageable and not all doom and gloom. There have been moments of laughter and hilarity, and this has always kept me going. Positivity and a smile can make even the dullest day bright.

In the last 10 months, I've found myself completely re-evaluating my life, family, friends, work and leisure. I've learnt to rewire my brain to not think or dwell on anything too painful. If I find myself drifting into feeling sorry for myself territory, I try to bring myself back by thinking of all the positive things that have happened. This has been an incredibly tough journey for me, and for those closest to me, but we have done it and now it's time to carry on with my life story.

P.S. If you'd like to see more photos from this incredible journey, go to: debbiesdiaryblog.wordpress.com

# Ꞔpilogue

## May 2017

I wrote the final entry to my blog back in February, but, for some reason, held on to it and didn't publish it.

My first annual mammogram came back clear, and the first year check-up with the consultant was also very positive. My family were over the moon to hear the news, and my mum was ready to crack open a bottle of fizz to celebrate.

The sad thing is, it never happened.

Mum & Dad 60th wedding anniversary

My darling mum passed away on 2 May 2017 as a result of an infection following open heart surgery. She was a tower of strength throughout my treatment, and she pulled me through some of my darker days. I am heartbroken that she's gone and there will never be another to replace her, but she has taught me well, and I will strive to carry on with a positive attitude and a smile on my face.

May God bless my mum.

# About the Author

Hi, my name is Debbie Paton, and I'm now 53 years old and grateful for every day I'm still here on the planet.

I've been married to Gus for almost 25 years, and we have two beautiful daughters, Georgia (aged 19) and Phoebe (aged 16).

I grew up in Northamptonshire and though I've lived in many other locations, I settled back in Northamptonshire 19 years ago.

I spent much of my working life as a florist. I owned my own flower shop, taught floristry in agricultural colleges and managed a flower wholesaler. I retrained as a counsellor when the girls were young, and for the past decade or so, I've worked in the field of substance misuse. I enjoy a challenge!

In my spare time, I enjoy walking our two Parson Jack Russells, Fizz and Dave. I like to keep fit and regularly play badminton, practise yoga and dead lifting.

I love to travel and see new places. I'm always on the lookout for the next adventure.

My favourite pastime is to spend time with my family and our large circle of friends. These are the people who got me through the rough times, and I will be forever grateful to them.

I have never written before, so I'm apprehensive about how this will be received. However, if you read the book, you'll see that until very recently, I'd never done a lot of things. I grab life and opportunities eagerly these days. I'm going to make sure I squeeze every drop out of life. I love my life and I'm not ready to leave it yet.

Printed in Great Britain
by Amazon